1634
Published in the USA 1995 by JG Press
Distributed by World Publications, Inc
Copyright © 1994 by Colour Library Books Ltd, Godalming, Surrey
All rights reserved
No part of this book may be reproduced or transmitted in any
form or by any means, electronic or mechanical, including
photocopying, recording, or by any information storage and
retrieval system, without permission in writing from the Publisher.
Printed and Bound in Singapore
ISBN 1–57215–020–3

The JG Press imprint is a trademark of JG Press, Inc.
455 Somerset Avenue
North Dighton, MA 02764

Text by
Denise Jarrett-Macauley

DELICIOUS DESSERTS

JG
PRESS

Contents

Introduction

The most important thing about desserts is to make sure that they complement the rest of the meal. This book aims to provide you with a selection ranging from the simplest fruit dishes for summer meals – such as Melons and Mango on Ice – to hot, winter desserts, such as Apricot Pudding.

Chapter headings, with the exception of 'Special Desserts' and 'Quick Desserts', trace the seasons and reflect the availability of fruits throughout the year. Starting with spring, when not many fruits are available fresh, dishes like Savarin Chantilly and Coffee Pecan Pie make use of ingredients that are available all year round, such as tinned fruit and nuts. Meanwhile, Linzertorte could be a chance to use frozen fruit, and Lemon and Orange Chiffon Tart to use traditional winter and spring fare.

Summer is a time for fresh fruit and cool ices. Sherbets and granitas provide a refreshing and colourful method of serving fruits and their juices. These dishes are easy to make in advance and serve as unusual treats; together with a range of ice creams there is something for every taste and occasion.

Autumn heralds an abundance of fruits, such as plums, pears and apples. All these can be bottled and used in dishes like Honey Plum Cobbler, Pear and Nut Crêpes or Apple Dumplings with Walnut Sauce. Many of the dishes in this section are light, but warming. Red Crumble and Cherry Clafoutis are ideal for chillier, autumn days.

The thought of steamed and suet-based puddings is undeniably linked with winter, with Apple Betty filled with spices and Carrot Pudding served with hot custard on the menu. For the Christmas table a selection of puddings and desserts – such as flaming Yuletide Pudding, Snowballs, and a tangy Pacific Pudding served with orange butter – will set off the festive atmosphere.

Special occasions, of course, can arise at any time of the year and a variety of recipes has been included, some of which take time to prepare but produce spectacular results. Exotic fruits with puréed sauces and glamorously displayed, flaming dishes will provide a breathtaking end to any special meal.

As for the chapter on quick desserts, most of the recipes included can be made from ingredients to be found in one's larder or kitchen cupboard. Poor Knights of Windsor and Caramel Oranges are good examples of simple, easy-to-make dishes which can be made in 15 minutes.

Ingredients in the book are measured for 6 people.

Chocolate Lime Tart

PREPARATION TIME: 20 minutes

8oz graham crackers
3oz semi-sweet chocolate
2 tablespoons butter
12oz white marshmallows
⅔ cup milk
2 limes
⅔ cup heavy cream
2oz semi-sweet chocolate, grated
The grated rind of 1 lemon
⅔ cup heavy cream, whipped
  for decoration

Crush the cookies. Melt the chocolate and butter together and mix in the cookies. Lightly grease the sides and base of a 9 inch tart pan. Press the cooky mixture onto the base and sides of the dish. Melt the marshmallows in a basin over hot water and add the milk. Stir in the juice from one lime and grate the rind. Mix in the lemon rind, whip the heavy cream and fold into the marshmallow mixture. Pour into the crumb base and leave to set. Decorate the tart with the remaining cream, grated chocolate and slices of the second lime.

Cointreau and Mandarin Mousse

PREPARATION TIME: 10 minutes

10½oz can of mandarin oranges
1 tablespoon gelatin
4 tablespoons Cointreau or orange
  liqueur
3 egg yolks
2 tablespoons sugar

Strain the mandarins, reserving the juice. Sprinkle the gelatin over the juice. Pour two tablespoons of Cointreau over the mandarins and leave them to soak. Add the remaining Cointreau, egg yolks and sugar to the gelatin. Beat the egg mixture over a bowl of hot water until thick and frothy (with an electric beater this should take 4 minutes). Pour into individual glass dishes and chill until set. Spoon the soaked mandarins on top. Serve.

Cheese Mousse with Strawberries

PREPARATION TIME: 45 minutes

1 cup cottage cheese
5oz strawberries
3 tablespoons confectioners' sugar
2 tablespoons Cointreau or orange
  liqueur
2 tablespoons lemon juice
2 tablespoons orange juice
1 tablespoon gelatin
⅔ cup heavy cream
6 meringue rosettes

Chocolate Sauce

8oz chocolate
2 tablespoons milk
2 tablespoons butter

Put the cottage cheese into a bowl and add the strawberries, reserving a few strawberries for decoration. Sift the confectioners' sugar over the cheese and sprinkle over the Cointreau. Cover and leave to stand in the fridge for about half an hour. Heat the orange and lemon juice and dissolve the gelatin in it. Whilst the gelatin is still warm, stir in the cheese mixture. Stiffly whip the cream and fold it in. Serve the mousse on the plate and decorate with the reserved strawberries. Serve with some chocolate sauce and meringue rosettes.

Chocolate Sauce

Melt the chololate, milk and butter in a bowl over hot water. Stir rapidly. Serve.

This page: Chocolate Lime Tart.

Facing page: Cointreau and Mandarin Mousse (top) and Cheese Mousse with Strawberries (bottom).

Spring Desserts

Individual Banana Tarts

PREPARATION TIME: 30 minutes

COOKING TIME: 15 minutes

OVEN: 400°F

Pastry
1/3 cup butter
1½ cups flour
2 tablespoons sugar
1 egg yolk
1 tablespoon water

Filling
2 firm bananas
1 teaspoon lemon juice
2/3 cup heavy cream
Apricot jam to glaze

Pastry
Place the butter and flour into a bowl and rub to form a breadcrumb-like mixture. Stir in the sugar. Beat together the egg yolk and water and add to flour to form a stiff dough. Lightly knead and chill for ½ hour. Roll out pastry and cut using a 3 inch crimped cutter. Press into tartlet pans and bake until golden brown.

Filling
Slice the bananas and sprinkle with the lemon juice. Beat the cream and fill the pastry shells. Lay the sliced banana in a circle to cover the cream. Melt the apricot jam in a small saucepan and pour over tartlet pastry shells, making sure all the bananas are glazed. Serve cold.

Coffee Pecan Pie

PREPARATION TIME: 20 minutes
plus chilling

6oz graham crackers
1/3 cup butter, melted
2 tablespoons soft brown sugar
3/4 cup pecan nut halves
8oz marshmallows
1¼ cups strong black coffee
½oz gelatin
3 tablespoons hot water
2/3 cup heavy cream
1 teaspoon ground coffee

Crush the cookies and mix together with the butter and sugar.

Press the mixture onto the base and up the sides of a 7 inch springform cake pan. Chill. Reserve 8 halves of pecan nuts for decoration and chop the remainder. In a large saucepan dissolve the marshmallows in the coffee, heating gently and stirring frequently. Dissolve the gelatin in the hot water and stir into the marshmallow mixture. Leave to cool until almost set. Beat the cream until it peaks and fold into the coffee mixture. Add the chopped nuts. Pour onto the crushed cooky base and chill until set. Remove from the pan and decorate with the nut halves. Sprinkle with the ground coffee.

Savarin Chantilly

PREPARATION TIME: 35 minutes
plus chilling

COOKING TIME: 30 minutes

OVEN: 400°F

Savarin
1½ cups strong white flour
½ teaspoon salt
6 tablespoons milk
2 level teaspoons dried yeast
1 level teaspoon sugar
2 eggs
1/3 cup butter

Syrup
3/4 cup sugar
1¼ cups water
*Pared rind of ½ lemon and juice of
    1 lemon*
3 tablespoons rum

Filling
2/3 cup light cream
2/3 cup heavy cream
1lb canned or fresh fruit

Savarin
Butter and sprinkle with flour an 8 inch ring mold. Sift the flour and salt into a mixing bowl. Heat the milk in a small saucepan and add the dried yeast and sugar (do not boil the milk). Leave in a warm place for 20 minutes or until the mixture looks frothy. Mix the eggs into the yeast mixture and pour into the flour. Stir with a wooden spoon to form a smooth batter.

Melt the butter and allow it to cool slightly. Pour into the batter and stir. Pour the batter into the ring mold and spread evenly. Put the mold into a polythene bag but leave room for the mixture to rise. Leave in a warm place. When the mixture has risen to the top of the pan bake in a preheated oven for half an hour until golden brown and firm to the touch.

Syrup
While the savarin is baking, add the sugar and water to a saucepan and finely pare the lemon rind. Stir over a low heat until the sugar has dissolved. Bring the mixture to the boil and simmer for 5 minutes. Remove from the heat and add the lemon juice and rum. When the savarin has cooled in the pan for five minutes remove it from the pan. Wash and dry the baking mold and pour the hot syrup evenly round the mold. Replace the savarin so that it floats in the syrup.

Filling
The savarin will soak up the syrup so that it can be turned out. Turn out the savarin and refrigerate overnight. Place savarin on a serving dish and whip the light and heavy cream. Spoon into the center and top with fruit (apricot, mango, oranges or stoned cherries make a suitable decoration).

Mont Blanc

PREPARATION TIME: 20 minutes
plus chilling

COOKING TIME: 1¼ hours

OVEN: 250°F

2 egg whites
6oz sugar
1 teaspoon vanilla essence
1 cup heavy cream
1½ tablespoons confectioners' sugar
8oz can chestnut purée
1 tablespoon brandy
*1oz semi-sweet chocolate, grated or
    chopped nuts to decorate*

Beat the egg whites until they peak, adding the sugar and vanilla essence. Fill a pastry bag with the

meringue mixture and fit a ½ inch plain tip. Draw six circles 3 inches in diameter on a cooky sheet lined with non-stick silicone paper and cover with the meringue. Bake in a very cool oven until firm but not brown. Cool. Whip the cream until it peaks and fold in the confectioners' sugar. Mix the chestnut purée with the brandy and spoon the mixture into a pastry bag fitted with an 1/8 inch tip and decorate round the edge of the meringue bases. Top with cream and chocolate or nuts to decorate. Serve chilled.

Mango Soufflé

PREPARATION TIME: 20 minutes
plus chilling

1 tablespoon water
Juice of one lemon
1/3 cup sugar
½oz gelatin
3 eggs (separated)
1 mango peeled and stoned
2/3 cup heavy cream

To decorate
¼ cup toasted chopped nuts
2/3 cup heavy cream, whipped
Caramel chips (see quick garnishes)

Prepare a 5 inch freezerproof soufflé dish. Cut a double strip of lightly oiled wax paper 20 x 5 inches and tie securely round the dish. Put the water and lemon juice in a small pan and sprinkle in the gelatin. Heat to dissolve the gelatin and cool. Beat the egg yolks and sugar until thick. Purée the mango and mix with the gelatin into the egg mixture. Fold in the stiffly beaten egg white with cream. Pour into the prepared dish and chill.

To decorate
Carefully remove the paper and press the nuts into the sides. Decorate with whipped cream. Another method of decoration is to use caramel chips.

Red Fruit Compote

PREPARATION TIME: 10 minutes
plus chilling

½ cup granulated sugar
1¼ cups water
6oz redcurrants, stalks removed
8oz raspberries, hulled
8oz strawberries, hulled
2 tablespoons Cointreau or orange
   liqueur
Light cream

Boil the sugar and water in a pan
till the sugar dissolves. This should
take about 5 minutes. Remove
from heat and cool. Put all the
fruits in a serving dish and pour
over the Cointreau and leave to
stand for an hour and a half. Stir
carefully from time to time. Pour
the cold syrup over the fruits and
serve chilled with cream.

Individual Fruit Salad

PREPARATION TIME: 20 minutes
plus chilling

3 bananas
2 oranges
4oz strawberries
2oz redcurrants

Passion Fruit Sauce
3 passion fruits
3 tablespoons clear honey
Juice of one lime
2 tablespoons dark rum

Peel and slice horizontally the bananas and oranges. Hull and halve the strawberries and arrange on individual plates and chill.

Passion Fruit Sauce
Spoon out the seeds and flesh of the passion fruits and boil with the honey and lime juice. Add two tablespoons of dark rum and chill. Pour the passion fruit sauce over the fruit and serve. Decorate with the redcurrants.

Almond Cream Tart

PREPARATION TIME: 20 minutes
COOKING TIME: 35 minutes
OVEN: 400°F

Tart
¼ cup flour
¼ cup sugar
2 eggs

Filling
⅔ cup heavy cream
1 level tablespoon sieved confectioners sugar
3 tablespoons ground almonds
12oz strawberries, hulled and sliced; keep one whole strawberry for decoration

Glaze
3 tablespoons water
⅓ cup superfine sugar
Whipped cream and strawberry leaves (optional)

Tart
Grease an 8 inch pie pan. Line the base with a circle of wax paper. Sieve the flour into a bowl. Put the sugar and eggs into another bowl and beat for 12 minutes over a saucepan of hot water, off the heat. The mixture should thicken and pale. Remove from the pan and beat for another 5 minutes. If using an electric beater, omit the beating over hot water. Sieve the flour a little at a time over the mixture and fold in with a metal spoon. Pour mixture into prepared pan and cook in a hot oven until firm. When cooked, leave to cool in the pan for a few minutes then turn onto a wire rack.

Filling
Whip the cream stiffly, adding the confectioners' sugar slowly. Fold in the almonds and spoon this mixture into the pie shell. Arrange the strawberries on top.

Glaze
Place water and sugar in a pan and slowly bring to the boil. The sugar should be dissolved. Stir the rapidly boiling mixture constantly. Boil for 2 minutes. Allow the glaze to cool and brush over the strawberries. Decorate with whipped cream and strawberry leaves if available.

Red Fruit Compote (far left), Individual Fruit Salad with Passion Fruit Sauce (center) and Almond Cream Tart (left).

Petits Pots de Café

PREPARATION TIME: 10 minutes
plus cooling

3 tablespoons sugar
3 tablespoons butter
1½ tablespoons rum
3 teaspoons instant coffee powder
(granules should be crushed)
3 eggs, separated
½ cup heavy cream, whipped
Walnut halves

Mix the sugar, butter, rum and coffee in a bowl over a pan of hot water, and stir until melted. Add the egg yolks and mix well. Leave to cook for 5 minutes over the hot water and remove from the heat. When the mixture has cooled, beat the egg whites until stiff and fold into the coffee mixture. Spoon into individual ramekins and decorate with whipped cream and nuts if available.

Fruit Coupelles with Dried Fruit Compote

PREPARATION TIME: 20 minutes

COOKING TIME: 7 minutes

OVEN: 400°F

¾ cup dried apricots
⅓ cup dried apple
¾ cup prunes
⅓ cup raisins
⅓ cup white raisins
⅓ cup currants
2½ cups strong black coffee

Coupelles
2 egg whites
5 tablespoons sugar
½ cup flour
¼ cup butter, melted and cooled

Place all the fruit ingredients in a saucepan and cover with the coffee. Boil rapidly then reduce heat to simmer for 3 minutes. Pour into a bowl and leave to cool for at least 10 hours. Beat the egg whites until frothy. Add the sugar slowly. The mixture should be very stiff. Fold in the flour and melted butter. Grease a cooky sheet. Drop the mixture onto the cooky sheet to form 4 inch rounds (the mixture makes 8). Cook in a preheated moderate oven until the edges are golden brown. Remove from the cooky sheet one at a time. Mold over an inverted ramekin to form a cup shape. When set remove from

the dish and leave to cool on a wire rack. To serve fill the coupelles with the fruit compote.

Raspberry and Hazelnut Galette

PREPARATION TIME: 35 minutes

COOKING TIME: 20 minutes

OVEN: 375°F

1 cup hazelnuts, shelled
½ cup softened butter
⅓ cup sugar
1 egg yolk, lightly beaten
A few drops of vanilla essence
1½ cups flour
A pinch of salt
1¾ cups heavy cream
1 level tablespoon sugar
1lb raspberries, hulled

Lightly grease three cooky sheets and dust with flour. Roast the hazelnuts in a hot oven 425°F , or under the broiler until the skin is split. Rub off the skins using kitchen paper and chop the nuts finely. Beat the sugar and butter until fluffy and beat in the egg yolk

and vanilla essence. Sieve the flour and salt and stir into the mixture adding the hazelnuts. Knead the mixture till it forms a smooth dough. Wrap in plastic wrap and chill for 30 minutes. Divide the dough into 3 pieces and roll on a lightly floured surface to form 7 inch rounds. Place each round onto the previously greased cooky sheet. Cook one at a time in a moderately heated oven until lightly golden. Cut one round into 8 equal portions while still hot and leave the remaining 2 to cool for 10 minutes. Whip the cream until thick and add the sugar. Put half the mixture into a pastry bag and save eight raspberries for decoration. Mix the remaining berries with the cream. Carefully position one galette on a serving plate. Cover with raspberry cream mixture and top with the remaining galette. Decorate eight swirls of cream on top and arrange the galette triangles on their edges supported by the cream swirls. Decorate with the reserved raspberries.

Pears in Wine

PREPARATION TIME: 15 minutes
plus chilling

COOKING TIME: 30 minutes

1½ cups granulated sugar
⅔ cup water
6 large pears, peeled
1 cup dry red wine

Gently heat the sugar and water until the sugar has dissolved. Add the pears and cover. Then simmer for 15 minutes. Stir in the wine and continue to simmer uncovered for another 15 minutes. Remove the pears from the saucepan and arrange in a serving dish. Bring the wine syrup back to the boil until thick. Pour over the pears and allow to cool. Serve chilled.

Strawberry and Peach Heart

PREPARATION TIME: 20 minutes
plus chilling

3 passion fruit
½ cup white wine
⅓ cup sugar
3 tablespoons Cointreau or orange
liqueur
4oz strawberries, hulled
3 peaches, halved and stoned
3 tablespoons strawberry jam
3 kumquats
3 kiwi fruit
3 tablespoons clear honey
1 teaspoon lime juice

Poach the flesh with the seeds of the passion fruit in the white wine until just tender. Add the sugar and continue to poach for a further four minutes. Sieve the mixture. Add the Cointreau and the strawberries and leave to cool. In a large saucepan filled with boiling water quickly submerge the

This page: Mango Soufflé (top), Mont Blanc (center) and Petits Pots de Café (bottom).

Facing page: Raspberries and Hazelnut Galette (top), Fruit Coupelles with Dried Fruit Salad (center) and Pears in Wine (bottom).

peaches and halve, removing the stone. Sieve the strawberry jam and using a writing tip fill a pastry bag, and reserve in the refrigerator. Slice the kumquats. To make the kiwi fruit sauce, peel the kiwi fruit and purée them. Pass them through a sieve and stir in the honey and lime juice. Using the sieved strawberry jam reserved in pastry bag, make heart shapes on each of the individual plates making sure not to break the line of strawberry jam. Fill the outline with the fruit, placing the peach half to one side and fill the hole left by removing stone with the strawberries. Pour over the kiwi fruit sauce and decorate with leaves. Serve chilled.

Chocolate and Brandy Cheesecake

PREPARATION TIME: 30 minutes
plus chilling

COOKING TIME: 1 hour
OVEN: 325°F

6oz chocolate graham crackers
⅓ cup butter, melted
6oz chocolate
2 tablespoons brandy
2 eggs, lightly beaten
½ cup soft brown sugar
1½ cups cream cheese
2 tablespoons cornstarch

To decorate
Confectioners' sugar

Crush the crackers and mix them with the melted butter. Butter the sides and base of a loose-bottomed 7 inch cake pan. Spoon the biscuit mixture into the cake pan, press onto the sides and base, and refrigerate for half an hour. Melt 4oz of the chocolate in a heatproof bowl over a pan of water and stir in the brandy. Beat together the eggs and sugar until thick. Add the cheese and continue to beat until the mixture is soft. Stir in the melted chocolate and cornstarch.

Pour the mixture into the cake pan and stand it on a cooky sheet. Bake until it sets. Remove from the oven and cool, then chill for 4 hours before serving. To serve: remove the cheesecake from the cake pan and grate the remaining chocolate on top. Sift with a little confectioners' sugar and serve.

Peach Brûlée

PREPARATION TIME: 20 minutes
BROILER SETTING: high

8 egg yolks
⅓ cup sugar
2½ teaspoons vanilla essence
6 peach halves, canned or fresh
⅓ cup soft brown sugar
Heavy cream

Beat the egg yolks and sugar until smooth and thick. Beat in the cream and pour the mixture into a saucepan. Cook over a low heat. Stir frequently until the mixture is

This page: Summer Pudding (left) and Strawberry and Peach Heart (right).

Facing page: Apricot Cream Cheese Dessert (top left), Peach Brûlée (top right) and Chocolate Brandy Cheesecake (bottom).

thick enough to coat the back of a wooden spoon. Beat for 2 minutes off the heat. Stir in the vanilla essence and pour the mixture into a heatproof serving dish. When cool, arrange the peach halves on top of the sauce (cut side down). Chill for 1 hour. Sprinkle the soft brown sugar over the peaches and place the dish under a hot broiler. When the sugar melts and starts to caramelize remove the dish from the broiler and serve at once.

Summer Pudding

PREPARATION TIME: 10 minutes
plus chilling

1lb 8oz fresh soft fruit
3/4 cup granulated sugar
9 slices of white bread (use thick
   slices and remove the crusts)
Whipped cream

Put all the fruit into a saucepan
with the sugar and heat until the
sugar is dissolved. Shake the pan so
that the fruit will stay whole.
Remove from heat and cool. Line
the base and sides of a 1¾ pint
pudding mold with the slices of
bread, trying not to leave any gaps.
Pour the fruit juice into the center
of the pudding and cover the top
completely with bread and press
down firmly. Place a saucer or small
plate on top of the pudding and
weigh down. Chill in the fridge
overnight. Turn out and decorate
with whipped cream.

Almond Pear

PREPARATION TIME: 20 minutes
plus chilling

COOKING TIME: 1 hour

OVEN: 300°F

2½ cups heavy cream
6 egg yolks
¼ cup sugar
½ teaspoon almond essence
½ cup granulated sugar
⅔ cup water
4 large pears peeled, stoned and
   sliced thinly
¾ cup soft brown sugar
Lemon juice to sprinkle on pears

Pour the cream into a saucepan and
heat (do not allow the cream to
boil). Put the egg yolks, sugar and
almond essence into a bowl and
stir well. Slowly pour into the

heated cream. Pour the mixture
into a 1¾ pint baking dish and
stand the dish in a roasting pan half
filled with water (this is known as a
bain marie). Loosely cover with foil
and bake until set. Remove the
dish from the bain marie and leave
until cold. Refrigerate overnight.
Put the granulated sugar and water
in a saucepan and heat gently until
the sugar has dissolved. Bring to
the boil until thick and golden in
color. Oil a shallow cake pan and
pour the caramelized sugar in.
When the caramel has set, crack
into small pieces with a rolling pin.
Arrange the pear slices on top of
the baked cream and sprinkle with
soft brown sugar, and lemon juice.
Broil until the sugar has dissolved
and the juice is bubbling. Leave to
cool and return to the fridge for
half an hour. Sprinkle with caramel
chips before serving.

Apricot Cream Cheese Dessert

PREPARATION TIME: 20 minutes
plus chilling

BROILER SETTING: high

8oz crushed English rolled wafers
½ teaspoon ground ginger
½ cup butter, melted
2 cups cream cheese
¼ cup sugar
½ cup light cream
2 tablespoons lemon juice
1 tablespoon gelatin dissolved in
   2 tablespoons hot water
1lb can of apricot halves, drained
2oz preserved stem ginger, drained
   and chopped
1¾ cups heavy cream
¼ cup soft brown sugar

Grease a 9 inch loose-bottomed
cake pan with a little butter. In a
large mixing bowl crush the English
rolled wafers, ground ginger and

butter and spoon into the base of
the cake pan, pressing down with
the back of a spoon. Place the
cream cheese and sugar into a bowl
and beat with a wooden spoon
until the mixture is smooth. Stir in
the light cream, lemon juice and
dissolved gelatin. Beat well so that
all the mixture is blended together.
Spoon the mixture into the pan
and refrigerate for 40 minutes.
When the filling is set, remove the
pan and arrange the apricot halves
on top of the filling. Sprinkle over
the preserved ginger and soft
brown sugar. Broil for three
minutes until the sugar has
caramelized. Remove the dessert
from the pan and serve.

Orange and Lemon Chiffon Tart

PREPARATION TIME: 45 minutes

COOKING TIME: 20 minutes

OVEN: 400°F

Pastry Shell
1½ cups flour
Pinch of salt
7 tablespoons butter
2 tablespoons sugar
1 egg yolk

Filling
3 eggs, separated
⅓ cup sugar
2 large oranges
1 large lemon
1 tablespoon gelatin
Warm water

For decoration
Sliced orange and lemon fan
⅔ whipped cream

Pastry Shell
Sieve the flour and salt into a bowl
and cut in the fat. Add the sugar
and mix well. Mix to a stiff paste
with the egg yolk to form a pliable

dough. Turn onto a floured board
and roll out. Use to line an 8 inch
pie ring. Cut a circle from non-stick
silicone baking paper and lay on
top of pastry. Sprinkle with baking
beans or crusts of bread (baking
blind). Bake for about 20 minutes
at 400°F. Remove the baking beans
and paper and return to the oven
for 5 minutes.

Filling
Beat the egg yolks, sugar and grated
rind of two oranges and one lemon
until thick. Dissolve the gelatin in a
little warm water and make up to
1¼ cups) with orange juice and
water. Pour the gelatin mixture into
the egg mixture and beat until it
starts to thicken. Lightly fold in the
stiffly beaten egg white, pile into
the pie shell and leave to set.
Decorate with whipped cream and
slices of orange.

Gateau American

PREPARATION TIME: 10 minutes

COOKING TIME: 20 minutes

OVEN: 400°F

⅓ cup granulated sugar
1 tablespoon butter
⅓ cup breadcrumbs
3 eggs, beaten
¾lb stoned dates
⅓ cup walnuts, chopped
1¾ cups whipped cream
Nuts

Mix the sugar, butter and breadcrumbs with the beaten eggs, dates
and walnuts. Cook in a shallow
pan until cooked (20 minutes).
When cold, crumble with a fork.
Layer fruit mixture and stiffly
whipped cream in tall glasses and
top with a rosette of whipped
cream. Decorate with a nut.

Facing page: Almond Pear (top), Gateau American (right) and Orange and Lemon Chiffon Tart (bottom).

Summer Desserts

Gooseberry Pie

PREPARATION TIME: 20 minutes

COOKING TIME: 1 hour

OVEN: 425°F for 30 minutes, then 350°F for 30 minutes

Pastry
2½ cups flour
Pinch of salt
5 tablespoons butter (cut into small pieces)
5 tablespoons lard (cut into small pieces)
2½ tablespoons cold water

Filling
2lb gooseberries, topped and tailed
1 cup granulated sugar
Milk to glaze or beaten egg
Light cream or custard

Pastry
Sift the flour with the salt. Add the fat and mix until it resembles breadcrumbs. Stir in the water and form into a firm dough. Roll out half the pastry on a lightly floured surface and use it to line an 8 inch quiche pan or pie pan.

Filling
Mix the gooseberries with the sugar and fill the lined pie pan. Roll out the remaining pastry and cover the pie. Dampen the edges and seal together. Any excess pastry can be used to make leaves to decorate. Make a small hole in the center of the pie and brush the pastry with milk or beaten egg. Place on cooky sheet and cook in a hot oven. Serve with light cream or custard.

Melons and Mangoes on Ice

PREPARATION TIME: 1¼ hours

1 medium size Ogen melon
2 large mangoes

Slice melon in half and scoop out flesh in balls. Peel mangoes and slice. Mix mango slices and melon balls together and arrange in a glass bowl. Chill for 1 hour.

Frozen Gooseberry Fool

PREPARATION TIME: 20 minutes plus freezing

COOKING TIME: 15 minutes

1½lb gooseberries
⅔ cup water
Sprig of mint
¾ cup sugar
A little green food coloring
⅔ cup heavy cream, lightly whipped

Top and tail gooseberries. Place in a pan with the water and mint. Cover and simmer for approximately 15 minutes or until soft. Take off the heat and stir in the sugar until dissolved, then add food coloring. Take out the sprig of mint. Sieve and ensure all pips are removed. Cool and blend with the cream. Place in container and freeze.

Brown Bread Ice Cream

PREPARATION TIME: 20 minutes plus freezing

2 cups plus 3 tablespoons vanilla ice cream
4 small slices brown bread
1 teaspoon ground cinnamon
½ cup water
⅓ cup sugar

Put the ice cream into a large mixing bowl and break it up, allowing it to soften. Cut the crusts from the bread and discard. Crumble the slices into a bowl, adding the ground cinnamon, reserve. Put the water and sugar into a small saucepan and stir until the sugar has dissolved. Boil until the mixture caramelizes and turns brown. Remove from the heat and stir in the breadcrumbs and cinnamon mixture. Blend the mixture into the ice cream, making sure the breadcrumbs do not form large lumps. Turn the mixture into a rigid container for freezing, (leave ½ inch space at the top of the container). Freeze the mixture and serve.

Brown Bread Ice Cream (top left), Melons and Mangoes on Ice (top right), Frozen Gooseberry Fool (bottom left) and Gooseberry Pie (bottom right).

Cherry 'Spoom'

PREPARATION TIME: 20 minutes
plus freezing

1 cup plus 2 tablespoons sugar
1¼ cups water
Juice of 2 limes
2 fresh peppermint leaves
2½ cups Sauternes
3 egg whites
Cherry brandy

Boil ¼ cup of the sugar with the
water, lime juice and peppermint
leaves. Leave to cool and strain
into the Sauternes. Freeze the
sherbet. Beat the egg whites and
add the remaining sugar until it
peaks. Remove the sherbet from
the freezer and beat in the
meringue mixture. Serve in glasses
and pour over the cherry brandy.

Apple and White Raisin and Brandy Ice

PREPARATION TIME: 10 minutes
plus soaking and freezing time

2½ cups apple juice
¼ cup sugar
1¼oz packet dried apple flakes
¾ cup white raisins
A few drops green food color
1 egg white, stiffly beaten

Put the apple juice in a pan with
sugar. Heat gently until the sugar
has dissolved. Boil quickly for 5
minutes and remove from heat.
Cool. Soak apple flakes and white
raisins in brandy and add enough
apple syrup to cover mixture. Soak
for 4 hours. Then mix apple, white
raisins and brandy adding a few
drops of food color mixture with
the remaining apple syrup in a
shallow container and freeze. Mash
with a fork and fold in egg whites.
Return to the freezer. Serve frozen
in glasses.

**This page: Burgundy Granita
(top), Apple and White
Raisin and Brandy Ice
(center) and Champagne
Granita (bottom).**

**Facing page: Cherry 'Spoom'
(top), Raspberry Malakoff
(center) and Cherry
Cinnamon Sherbet (bottom).**

Burgundy Granita

PREPARATION TIME: 15 minutes
plus freezing

⅓ cup sugar, plus 2 tablespoons
Juice of ½ lime and ½ orange
1 tablespoon water
Small bunch lemon balm leaves
½ bottle good Burgundy
½ cup heavy cream
Blackberries to decorate

Boil half the sugar with the lime and orange juice and water, and the balm leaves. Cool, strain and add to Burgundy. Freeze in a shallow container. To serve: whip the cream with the remaining sugar. Scrape the granita with a spoon to produce ice shavings and serve shavings into glasses, decorate with cream and blackberries.

Champagne Granita

PREPARATION TIME: 5 minutes
plus freezing time

⅔ bottle champagne
Fresh blackcurrants and raspberries
Superfine sugar to dust

Freeze the champagne in a shallow container. When frozen, scrape off and serve into glasses. Decorate with blackcurrants and raspberries. Dust with superfine sugar.

Raspberry Malakoff

PREPARATION TIME: 35 minutes
plus chilling

¾ cup sugar
¾ cup butter
1¼ cups heavy cream
¾ cup ground almonds
3 tablespoons kirsch
8oz fresh raspberries
1 packet ladyfingers
Whipped cream

Beat the sugar and butter until fluffy. Whip the cream until it peaks and fold in the ground almonds. Add the kirsch and raspberries. Mix the sugar and butter with the cream fruit mixture. Line a 7 inch cake pan with non-stick silicone paper. Stand the ladyfingers round the sides of the cake pan with the sugary side outermost. Spoon the malakoff mixture into the middle and press it down. Make sure the top is smooth. Refrigerate until the malakoff feels firm. With a sharp knife, trim the cookies to the same level as the malakoff mixture. Turn the malakoff out upside down. Decorate with whipped cream if desired. Serve chilled.

Cherry Cinnamon Sherbet

PREPARATION TIME: 25 minutes
plus freezing

1¼ cups plus 1 tablespoon sugar
1¼ cups water
1 piece cinnamon stick
18oz fresh sour cherries
Juice of ½ lemon
1 cup heavy cream
Seeds of ¼ vanilla pod
Fresh cherries

Boil 1¼ cups of the sugar for 3 minutes in water and cinnamon and leave to cool. Remove the cinnamon sticks and stone the cherries. Purée the cherries and stir in the lemon juice. Mix with the sugar syrup and freeze. Flavor the cream with the tablespoon of sugar and vanilla. Whip until thick. Put the sherbet into individual glasses and decorate with cream and cherries.

Strawberry Alaska

PREPARATION TIME: 10 minutes
COOKING TIME: 2-3 minutes
OVEN: 275°F

1 shop-bought strawberry jam jelly-roll
Soft-scoop strawberry ice cream to cover

Meringue
2 egg whites
½ cup superfine sugar

Cover jelly-roll with ice cream. Return to freezer. Beat egg whites until they form stiff peaks. Beat in half the sugar. Then fold in the rest. Remove ice cream covered jelly-roll from freezer and cover with meringue mixture. Place in oven and cook meringue until just turning golden. (Approximately 2-3 minutes.) Serve immediately.

Strawberry Yogurt Ice

PREPARATION TIME: 20 minutes
plus freezing

8oz fresh or thawed, frozen strawberries
1¼ cups plain low fat yogurt
2 teaspoons gelatin
2 tablespoons water
1 egg white
5 tablespoons superfine sugar
A few strawberries

Blend strawberries and yogurt until smooth. Sprinkle gelatin over the water in a small bowl. Place bowl in a pan of hot water until the gelatin is dissolved. Cool slightly and add to the strawberry mixture. Pour into the container and freeze until icy round the edges. Put mixture into bowl and beat until smooth. In another bowl beat the egg white stiffly, carefully adding the sugar, and fold into strawberry mixture. Pour back into container and freeze. To serve – scoop into glasses and decorate with strawberries.

Peach Melba

PREPARATION TIME: 10 minutes

1 large can peaches (2 halves per person)
2 scoops ice cream per person
Chocolate sauce or raspberry purée
Flaked almonds

Place 2 scoops of ice cream per serving in individual bowls. Place 2 peach halves on top. Serve with chocolate sauce or raspberry purée. Decorate with flaked almonds.

Lemon Sherbet

PREPARATION TIME: 15 minutes
plus freezing

Grated rinds and juice of 2 lemons
Cold water
⅓ cup sugar
1 teaspoon gelatin
2 egg whites

Mix the lemon juice and rind with cold water to make 3 cups of fluid. Put the liquid in a saucepan with the sugar and boil. Remove from the heat and beat in the gelatin. Pour into a mixing bowl and place in the freezer until it begins to harden. Beat the egg whites until stiff and beat them into the lemon mixture. Return to the freezer, leaving a ½ inch head space in the container.

Pastel Coupé

PREPARATION TIME: 35 minutes
plus freezing

Yellow
2½ cups water
2 level teaspoons gelatin
1¼ cups superfine sugar
3 lemons
2 egg whites

Green
2½ cups water
2 level teaspoons gelatin
1 cup sugar
2 lemons
2 egg whites
2 tablespoons crème de menthe

Yellow
Measure out two tablespoons of water and sprinkle with gelatin. Place the remaining water and sugar in a saucepan. Add pared lemon rinds and stir over the heat until the sugar has dissolved. Bring to the boil and simmer for 5 minutes. Remove from heat and add gelatin mixture. Dissolve completely and stir in the lemon juice. Leave to cool. Strain the mixture into a container and freeze until partially frozen. Place in chilled mixing bowl and beat with beaten egg whites until thick and snowy. Return to container and freeze.

Green
For the green pastel coupé use basic method and ingredients as listed. Add the crème de menthe with lemon juice. To serve: use an ice-cream scoop, take half the green and half the yellow into one scoop. Serve in meringue cases or glasses.

Facing page: Strawberry yogurt Ice (top), Peach Melba (center) and Strawberry Alaska (bottom).

Curaçao Granita with Champagne

PREPARATION TIME: 10 minutes
plus freezing

⅓ cup sugar
⅔ cup water
Juice of 1 lime
Juice of 1 orange
3 tablespoons blue Curaçao
⅔ bottle champagne

Boil half the sugar with the water, lime and orange juice for two to three minutes. Cool, strain, add to the Curaçao and the champagne. Pour into a flat freezer-proof container and freeze. To serve: scrape with a spoon and serve in glasses.

Blackcurrant Sherbet

PREPARATION TIME: 20 minutes
plus freezing

2lb fresh or thawed, frozen
   blackcurrants
1 cup plus 2 tablespoons sugar
1¼ cups water
2 egg whites

Put all the ingredients except the egg whites into a saucepan. Heat slowly and cook for 15 minutes. Rub the fruit mixture through a sieve and pour into a freezer-proof container with a lid. Freeze until mushy. Beat the egg whites until firm and fold into the mixture. Return to the freezer.

Inset illustration: (from top to bottom) Curaçao Granita with Champagne, Lemon Sherbet, Pastel Coupé and Blackcurrant Sherbet.

Ginger Syllabub

PREPARATION TIME: 15 minutes

4oz jar preserved ginger
2½ cups heavy cream, lightly
　whipped

Chop 2 pieces of the ginger and mix into the cream along with 2 tablespoons of the syrup. Serve in glasses or bowls and decorate with sliced ginger. Chill until ready to serve.

Apricot Ice Roll

PREPARATION TIME: 35 minutes
plus freezing

COOKING TIME: 12 minutes

OVEN: 425°F

Sponge mixture
2 eggs
¼ cup sugar
½ cup flour

Filling and decorating
4 tablespoons apricot jam
2½ cups soft-scoop ice cream (vanilla)
Cream to decorate
Dried apricots, thinly sliced

Beat eggs and sugar until light and fluffy. Carefully fold in flour. Turn into a greased and floured jelly-roll pan and bake. Turn out onto a clean cloth and leave to cool. Spread sponge with apricot jam and softened ice cream. Roll up using clean cloth. Place in freezer until ice cream is hardened. Decorate with cream and sliced apricots.

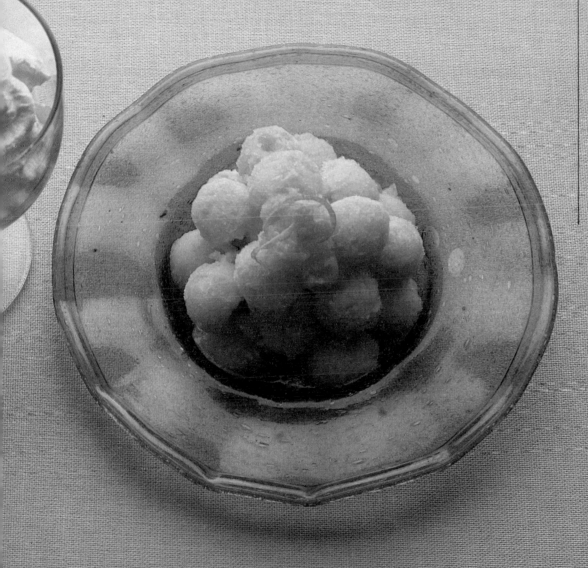

Mango Sherbet

PREPARATION TIME: 15 minutes
plus freezing

1 cup mango purée
Juice of ½ lime
⅔ cup dry white wine
⅔ cup mineral water
1 egg white
¼ cup sugar

Mix the mango purée with the lime juice, white wine and mineral water. Beat the egg white until it peaks and slowly add the sugar. Fold the egg white into the mango mixture and freeze.

Apricot Ice Roll (far left), Ginger Syllabub (center) and Mango Sherbet (left).

Banana Ice Crêpes

PREPARATION TIME: 30 minutes

12 cooked crêpes
2 large bananas
12 scoops soft-scoop vanilla ice
   cream
Chocolate sauce

Mash one banana, and combine with ice cream. Fold the crêpes in half and place on individual plates. Fill crêpes with the mixture of banana and ice cream. Decorate with other sliced banana. Serve with chocolate sauce.

Mousse Glacée au Chocolat

PREPARATION TIME: 20 minutes
plus freezing

4 egg yolks
2 tablespoons sugar
3 teaspoons vanilla essence
1¼ cups heavy cream
2 egg whites, stiffly whipped
Chocolate sauce

Beat egg yolks and sugar until light and creamy. Add vanilla essence. Add the cream and egg whites. Freeze the mixture. Serve with chocolate sauce.

Chocolate Banana Ice

PREPARATION TIME: 35 minutes
plus freezing

⅔ cup milk
3 tablespoons sugar
3 tablespoons chocolate (broken into
   bits)
1 egg, beaten
1 teaspoon vanilla essence
⅔ heavy cream, whipped until soft
   peaking

Banana Cream
4 medium bananas
1 tablespoon lemon juice
3 tablespoons confectioners' sugar,
   sieved
⅔ cup heavy cream, beaten

Place the milk, sugar and chocolate in a saucepan and heat gently. Pour onto the beaten egg and stir constantly until mixed. Return the mixture to the saucepan and cook until the custard thickens. Strain

the mixture, add the vanilla essence and allow to cool. Fold the cream into the custard mixture. Beat rapidly and turn into a metal freezing container.

Banana Cream
Peel and chop the bananas and sprinkle with lemon juice. Dust the fruit with confectioners' sugar and fold the whipped cream in with the bananas. Stir the chocolate mixture with banana cream and freeze. Remove from freezer to fridge 20 minutes before serving.

Refreshing Sherbet

PREPARATION TIME: 15 minutes
plus freezing

⅓ cup sugar
1¾ cups water
3 ripe mangoes, peeled, stoned and
   mashed
Juice of 3 lemons
3 tablespoons white rum
3 egg whites, beaten

Over low heat, dissolve sugar in the water, boil for 10 minutes. Leave to cool. Blend mangoes with lemon juice and rum. Add the syrup. Pour into a container and freeze until just frozen. Turn into a bowl. Fold in the egg whites. Freeze.

Minted Lime Ice

PREPARATION TIME: 15 minutes
plus freezing

¾ cup sugar
1½ cups water
Grated rind and juice of 6 limes
4 tablespoons fresh mint, finely
   chopped
⅔ cup heavy cream
3 tablespoons light cream

Place the sugar and water in a saucepan. Stir gently over a low heat. When the sugar has dissolved bring the mixture to the boil. Remove the pan from the heat. Stir in the grated rind of the limes. Add the juice and stir in the mint. Let the mixture cool and pour into ice trays. Freeze the mixture, covered with foil. When the mixture is frozen, crush it. Lightly whip the creams together. Stir the lime ice into the cream and re-freeze. Slightly thaw and spoon into small glasses to serve.

Lemon Ice Cream Sponge

PREPARATION TIME: 20 minutes
plus freezing

COOKING TIME: 15 minutes

OVEN: 425°F

Sponge
3 large eggs
⅓ cup sugar
¾ cup flour, sieved
1 teaspoon baking powder

Filling
4 level teaspoons lemon curd
1 grated rind of lemon
6 scoops soft-scoop vanilla ice cream

To decorate
3 tablespoons heavy cream
Confectioners' sugar
Sugared lemon slices

Sponge
Beat eggs and sugar until light and fluffy. Sieve in flour and mix in carefully. Bake in a large 5 inch cooky sheet. Turn out and cool.

Filling
Slice the cake into three horizontally. On bottom and middle slices spread lemon curd. Mix together the lemon rind and vanilla ice cream. Spread on top of the lemon curd. Sandwich together and freeze.

To decorate
Whip cream until stiff; place in pastry bag with a star tip; decorate rosettes on top of the sponge. Dust with confectioners' sugar and add lemon slices.

Custard Ice Cream

PREPARATION TIME: 20 minutes

5 egg yolks
⅔ cup light cream
¾ cup sugar
1¼ cups heavy cream

Combine egg yolks, light cream and ½ cup of the sugar in a mold. Place over a pan of simmering water and stir until mixture coats the back of a spoon. Strain mixture into a bowl and leave to cool. Whip heavy cream lightly. Mix with custard carefully. Fold in remaining ¼ cup of sugar. Pour into a freezer-proof container. Cover and freeze.

Coconut Sherbet

PREPARATION TIME: 20 minutes
plus freezing

1 cup canned coconut juice
⅔ cup mineral water
2 tablespoons dark rum
2 egg whites
½ cup sugar

To decorate
2 bananas, sliced
Chocolate sauce

Mix the coconut juice with the mineral water and rum. Beat the egg whites until stiff, gradually adding the sugar. Stir the egg whites into the coconut mixture with a balloon whisk and freeze until creamy. Serve with banana slices and chocolate sauce.

Honey Ice Cream

PREPARATION TIME: 15 minutes
plus freezing

1lb raspberries
⅔ cup clear honey
⅔ cup heavy cream
2 tablespoons lemon juice
3 egg whites
½ cup water
⅔ cup light cream
4 tablespoons granulated sugar

Cook the raspberries in a saucepan with the honey and water. Add the sugar and cook for 5 minutes until dissolved. Leave to cool. Rub the mixture through a sieve and chill. Beat the heavy cream until thick and stir in the light cream. Fold the creams into the fruit mixture. Freeze until almost solid. Beat and re-freeze.

Facing page: Mocha Soufflé (top), Chocolate Banana Ice (center left), Banana Ice Crêpes (center right) and Mousse Glacée au Chocolat (bottom).

Fancy Ice

PREPARATION TIME: 15 minutes

COOKING TIME: 10 minutes

OVEN: 425°F

Sponge
2 eggs
¼ cup sugar
½ cup flour

Topping
1 cup confectioners' frosting
1 tablespoon lemon juice
A few drops yellow food color

Filling and decoration
Blackberry sherbet
Apricot purée
Blackberries

Sponge
Beat eggs and sugar until light and fluffy. Sieve in the flour, fold gently into mixture. Lightly grease and flour a muffin pan. Spoon into 12 portions and bake until golden brown. Turn out and cool on a wire rack.

Topping
Melt the confectioners' frosting. Add the lemon juice and food coloring. Spoon over the cakes, leave to harden and set.

Filling and decoration
Fit a star tip on a pastry bag and fill with blackberry sherbet. Cut sponges in half, swirl sherbet on top of the base then sandwich with the remaining half of sponge. Serve with a spoonful of apricot purée on the side and decorate with blackberries.

Mocha Soufflé

PREPARATION TIME: 30 minutes
plus chilling

½oz gelatin
4 tablespoons warm water
3 tablespoons cocoa
1 teaspoon instant coffee
1¾ cups milk
4 eggs, separated
⅓ cup sugar
2 tablespoons rum
⅔ cup fresh heavy cream, whipped
Chocolate curls

Dissolve the gelatin in a small mold with the warm water. Mix the cocoa and coffee with the milk and bring to the boil in a saucepan. In a mixing bowl beat the egg yolks and

sugar together until pale and fluffy. Gradually beat in the milk mixture. Place the bowl over a saucepan of hot water for 15 minutes. Stir gently. Remove from heat and stir in the rum and dissolved gelatin. Allow to cool. Beat the egg whites until they peak and fold into the mixture. Mix in half of the heavy

cream. Pour into a prepared 2½ cups soufflé dish. Chill until set. Decorate with the remaining whipped cream and chocolate curls.

This page: Fancy Ice (top), Custard Ice-Cream (center) and Coconut Sherbet (bottom). Facing page: Refreshing Sherbet (top), Minted Lime Ice (center left), Honey Ice-Cream (center right) and Lemon Ice-Cream Sponge (bottom).

Autumn Desserts

Illustrations below: Charlotte (left), Steamed Chocolate Pudding with Rum Sauce (center) and Viennoise Pudding with German Sauce (right).

Charlotte

PREPARATION TIME: 30 minutes

COOKING TIME: 40 minutes

OVEN: 350°F

1lb tart apples
½ cup white breadcrumbs
¼ cup shredded suet
⅓ cup brown sugar
1 lemon
Superfine sugar for topping
Custard or cream

Wash, peel, core and slice the apples. Mix together the breadcrumbs, suet, sugar and grated lemon rind. Sprinkle a little of this mixture in the bottom of a greased pie dish. Then add a layer of apple slices (sprinkled with juice from the lemon) and fill the dish with alternate layers of the breadcrumb mixture and sliced apples – finishing with a layer of breadcrumbs. Bake in the oven for 40 minutes. Turn out onto a hot dish and sprinkle lightly with superfine sugar. Serve with custard or cream.

Steamed Chocolate Pudding with Rum Sauce

PREPARATION TIME: 25 minutes

COOKING TIME: 1½ hours or until firm to touch

3oz cooking chocolate
Few drops of vanilla essence
⅓ cup butter
¾ cup sugar
3 eggs
2¼ cups flour
2 teaspoons baking powder
7½ tablespoons milk

Sauce

3 tablespoons cornstarch
1¾ cups milk
3 tablespoons sugar
3 tablespoons dark rum

Put the chocolate, vanilla and butter in a heatproof bowl placed over a pan of hot water. Heat gently, stirring to melt the chocolate and butter. When melted remove from the heat and cool. Stir the sugar into the chocolate mixture and beat in the eggs. Sift the flour and baking powder and mix in well. Stir in the milk. Grease a 2½ pint pudding mold. Pour the mixture into the pudding mold. Cover with a foil lid tied on securely with string. Steam pudding for 1½ hours.

Sauce

In a saucepan dissolve the cornstarch in the milk. Stir in the sugar and heat gently, stirring constantly. Bring the mixture to the boil and then reduce heat and simmer until it thickens and is smooth. Stir in the rum. Turn out the pudding and serve hot with sauce.

Viennoise Pudding with German Sauce

PREPARATION TIME: 60 minutes

COOKING TIME: 90 minutes

1oz sugar cubes
1 tablespoon water
1¼ cups milk
6oz bread
Grated rind of 1 lemon
⅔ cup white raisins
1½oz chopped candied peel
3 eggs
½ wineglass of sherry
⅓ cup superfine sugar

Sauce

2 egg yolks
⅔ cup sherry
1 tablespoon sugar
Strips of lemon rind

Using a thick pan, dissolve the sugar in a tablespoonful of water. Heat gently until dissolved, then bring to the boil and boil rapidly until the syrup turns brown. Heat the milk and pour over the syrup. Remove the crusts from the bread, then cut the bread into small cubes. Add the lemon rind, white raisins and candied peel. Beat the eggs and add the milk/syrup mixture to the eggs. Then add the sherry and superfine sugar. Pour the whole mixture over the bread and leave to soak for 30 minutes. Transfer to a greased mold, cover with greased foil and steam for 60-90 minutes until firm.

Sauce

Beat the egg yolks, warm the sherry and then mix together with the sugar and lemon rind. Sit the mold in a pan of hot water and beat thoroughly for 10 minutes. Do not over-heat the sauce or it will curdle. Serve immediately.

Crêpes

1 cup flour
Pinch of salt or sugar (for extra sweetness)
1 egg, lightly beaten
1¼ cups milk
1 teaspoon vegetable oil

Before doing any of the following pancake recipes, follow these instructions for making the crêpes. This mixture makes 12 crêpes. You can also buy them ready made.

Sieve the flour and salt into a bowl. Make a well in the center and break an egg into it with half the milk. Beat well, then when smooth add the remaining milk. Leave the mixture to stand for 40 minutes. Grease the skillet and heat it a little. Pour the batter into the skillet. Quickly tilt and rotate the skillet so the batter coats the bottom and pour off the excess batter. Cook over a moderate heat until the underside of the crêpe is gently brown. Turn crêpe over and brown the other side. Turn onto wax paper and keep warm.

"Sissi" Crêpes

PREPARATION TIME: 25 minutes
COOKING TIME: 20 minutes
OVEN: 400°F

6oz almond paste
3 tablespoons sugar syrup
3 tablespoons lemon juice
1½ tablespoons kirsch
2 tablespoons softened butter
6 tablespoons strawberry sauce
6 tablespoons Advocaat
6 scoops vanilla ice cream
Whipped cream

Mix the almond paste with the sugar syrup, lemon juice and kirsch and beat until fluffy. Divide the mixture between the crêpes and roll or fold them. Spread with butter, put in ovenproof dish and

heat through at oven temperature 400°F for five minutes. Put them on small plates and pour over strawberry sauce and liqueur. Serve with whipped cream and vanilla ice cream.

Chocolate Crêpes

OVEN: 400°F

6oz cherry jam
10 tablespoons softened butter
⅔ cup water
10 tablespoons sugar
4 tablespoons cocoa powder
3 tablespoons rum
6oz semi-sweet chocolate, chopped
6 tablespoons whipped cream

Fill the crêpes with the jam and roll or fold them. Spread them on top with half of the butter. Heat the crêpes for 5 minutes.

Sauce

In a saucepan boil up the water, sugar and the rest of the butter. Remove the pan from the heat and stir in the rum and chocolate. If the sauce is too thick, thin with light cream. Pour the hot sauce over the crêpes. Decorate with whipped cream.

Crêpes Suzette

PREPARATION TIME: 40 minutes
COOKING TIME: 35 minutes

Rind of 1 orange
6 lumps sugar
5 tablespoons butter
½ cup more sugar
¾ cup fresh orange juice
5 tablespoons orange liqueur
3 tablespoons brandy

Cream the ½ cup sugar and the butter till fluffy. Beat in the orange juice and rub the sugar cubes onto the rind so they look orange, reserve. Add the orange liqueur gradually. Spoon a little of the mixture into each pancake and roll or fold. Put the remaining mixture into a large skillet and place the crêpes on top. Scatter the sugar cubes on the top. Gently heat the skillet and melt the butter. In another saucepan warm the brandy and pour over the pancakes. Ignite the brandy and serve.

Pear and Nut Crêpes

PREPARATION TIME: 25 minutes
COOKING TIME: 15 minutes
OVEN: 350°F

12 cooked crêpes
¾ cup butter
½ cup confectioners' sugar
½ cup ground almonds
Few drops of almond essence
Grated rind of 1 lemon
26oz of canned pears, drained and sliced

Cream the butter and sugar together till the mixture is fluffy. Beat the ground almonds, almond essence and lemon rind into the mixture. Fold the pears carefully into the mixture. Divide the mixture between the crêpes and roll or fold each one. Arrange the crêpes in an ovenproof dish and re-heat gently in a moderate oven. Serve hot.

Apple and Nut Tart

PREPARATION TIME: 20 minutes
COOKING TIME: 40 minutes
OVEN: 425°F

1¼ cups flour
10 tablespoons sugar
Salt
1 egg
9 tablespoons butter, cut into pieces

Filling

1lb dessert apples, peeled, cored and sliced
¼ cup ground hazelnuts
1 teaspoon ground cinnamon
Juice of 1 lemon
3 tablespoons apricot brandy (optional)
½ cup apricot jam
½ cup chopped nuts

Pastry

Sift the flour and sugar (reserving 2 tablespoons of sugar for filling) and a pinch of salt into a mixing bowl. Make a well in the center and add the egg. Mix in the butter pieces, rub the ingredients to make a soft smooth dough. Rest the dough by leaving it in the fridge for 30 minutes. Grease an 8 inch pie dish. Roll out the pastry, line the dish.

Filling

Layer the apple and hazelnuts. Sprinkle with cinnamon and sugar,

lemon juice and apricot brandy. Put the apricot jam in a saucepan and heat until melted. Pour over filling. Sprinkle with the chopped nuts. Bake until golden and fruit is soft. Take tart out of oven and cool.

Treacle Tart

PREPARATION TIME: 25 minutes
COOKING TIME: 30 minutes
OVEN: 350°F

Pastry

1½ cups flour
Pinch of salt
3 tablespoons butter
3 tablespoons lard
Cold water to mix

Filling

1 cup corn syrup
¼ cup breadcrumbs
Lemon juice

Sieve the flour into a bowl. Add the salt and the lard to the flour. Chop the lard into small pieces with a knife and then rub into the flour with the fingertips. Add the water and mix to a stiff dough. Turn onto a lightly floured board and knead the dough until free from cracks. Roll out a little larger than a 9 inch pan. Line the edge of the pan with a strip of pastry (cut from the edge). Damp it well and then line the whole pan with the rolled out pastry. Seal the edges, trim off any excess pastry and decorate the edges.

Filling

Sprinkle the breadcrumbs into the lined pan and cover with corn syrup. Add a little lemon juice. Cut the remaining pastry trimmings into thin strips, twist, and lay across the tart. Bake for 30 minutes.

Facing page: Pear and Nut Crêpes (top left), Crêpes Suzette (top right), Chocolate Crêpes (center) and "Sissi" Crêpes (bottom).

Cherry Clafoutis

PREPARATION TIME: 15 minutes

COOKING TIME: 15 minutes

OVEN: 350°F

1½ cups milk
1 tablespoon dark rum
4 eggs
½ cup sugar
1 cup flour
Generous pinch of salt
14oz stoned cherries
Confectioners' sugar

Grease a shallow medium-sized baking dish. Place the milk, rum and eggs in a large mixing bowl and beat with a balloon whisk until smooth and frothy. Add the sugar a little at a time and beat till the sugar is dissolved. Add the flour, sift it a little at a time, mixing in the salt with the last spoonful. Pour half of the batter into the prepared dish and spread the cherries over the top, then pour the remaining batter over all the cherries. Bake until the pudding is firm in the center and sprinkle with a little confectioners' sugar. Serve hot.

Red Fruit Crumble

PREPARATION TIME: 15 minutes

COOKING TIME: 25 minutes with a further 15 minutes

OVEN: 375°F reduced to 350°F after 25 minutes

2 level teaspoons cornstarch
6 tablespoons granulated sugar
12oz raspberries, hulled
3 medium-sized ripe pears, peeled, quartered, cored and sliced.
1 cup flour
¼ cup margarine
¼ cup soft brown sugar
1 cup crunchy breakfast cereal, crushed
Custard or cream

In a large mixing bowl, mix the cornstarch and granulated sugar with the raspberries. Grease a 2½ pint ovenproof dish. Arrange the mixture alternately with the pears. Sieve into another bowl the flour and cut in the margarine. Crush the cereal and stir in with the soft brown sugar. Put all the mixture over the fruit and flatten, using the back of the spoon. Cook in a moderate oven, temperature 375°F for 25 minutes, then reduce the temperature to 350°F and cook

for 15 minutes until crumble is golden. Serve hot with custard or cream.

Honey Plum Cobbler

PREPARATION TIME: 30 minutes

COOKING TIME: 15 minutes plus a further 30 minutes

OVEN: 400°F

2lb ripe plums, halved and stoned
4-6 tablespoons clear honey
2 cups flour
2 teaspoons baking powder
2 tablespoons sugar
¼ cup butter
5-6 tablespoons milk
1 egg, beaten
Cream

Place the plums in an ovenproof dish with the honey, cover with a sheet of foil. Cook in a preheated oven for 15 minutes at 400°F. While the plums are cooking mix the flour, baking powder and sugar and cut in the butter. Using a knife stir in the milk and egg so the

mixture forms a soft dough. Lightly flour the work surface and roll out the dough. Cut with 2 inch cutter to form cobblers. Remove the plums from the oven and cool. Arrange the cobblers round the top of the dish overlapping slightly. Brush the top of each one with a little milk and sprinkle with sugar. Cook until golden. Serve hot with cream.

Les Bourdaines
(Apples Baked in Pastry)

PREPARATION TIME: 30 minutes

COOKING TIME: 20-25 minutes

OVEN: 325°F

3 cups flour
Pinch of salt
¾ cup butter
1½ tablespoons sugar
5-7 tablespoons iced water
6 large dessert apples, peeled and cored
6 tablespoons plum jam
1 egg, beaten, to glaze
Cream

Sift the flour and salt into a bowl. Rub in the butter until the mixture is like fine breadcrumbs. Stir in the sugar. Mix in enough water to give a smooth, pliable dough. Divide the dough into 6 pieces and roll out each square. Fill the centers of the apples with jam and place an apple on each pastry square. Brush the edges of the squares with water and wrap up the apples, sealing them well. Cut out some pastry leaves and decorate. Place on a cooky sheet. Brush the pastry with beaten egg, bake in a moderate pre-heated oven. Bake until golden brown. Serve hot with cream.

Alma Pudding with Wine Sauce

½ cup butter
2 tablespoons sugar
2 eggs
4 tablespoons flour
2 tablespoons orange marmalade
½ teaspoon bicarbonate of soda
⅓ cup milk

Wine Sauce
1 egg
⅔ cup sherry
1 tablespoon sugar

Beat butter and sugar until light. Add eggs and flour. Add the marmalade, bicarbonate of soda and milk. Place mixture in a pudding mold and cover with foil, tied in place with string. Place in a large pan, pour in hot water until it comes ¾ of the way up the mold. Bring water to the boil and steam for 1 hour. Remove and turn out into a serving plate and serve with wine sauce.

Wine Sauce
Combine ingredients. Place over a pan of boiling water. Beat until light and frothy. Serve.

This page: Red Fruit Crumble (top left), Cherry Clafoutis (top right) and Honey Plum Cobbler (bottom).

Facing page: Treacle Tart (top left), Les Bourdaines (top right), Apple and Nut Tart (center) and Alma Pudding (bottom).

Winter Desserts

Yorkshire Apple Tart

PREPARATION TIME: 30 minutes plus chilling

COOKING TIME: 25 minutes plus 15 minutes

OVEN: 375°F

10oz basic pastry
12oz tart apples, peeled, cored and
    sliced
2 tablespoons sugar
1 tablespoon water
Little milk and sugar to glaze
4oz strong cheese, sliced
Whipped cream

Roll out the pastry and use two-thirds to line an 8 inch pie ring. Fill the center with the sliced apples, sprinkle with sugar and water. Seal the edges, cover the tart with the remaining pastry, and brush the top with a little milk and sprinkle with sugar. Place in a preheated, moderately hot oven and bake for 20 to 25 minutes until the crust is firm and lightly browned. Leave to cool, then with care remove the crust with a sharp knife. Place the cheese on top of the apples. Replace the crust. Return to the oven and bake for 15 minutes until the cheese has melted. Serve hot with whipped cream. Serves 4 to 6.

Fruit Cobbler

PREPARATION TIME: 20 minutes

COOKING TIME: 20 minutes

OVEN: 450°F

2¼ cups flour
2 teaspoons baking powder
½ cup butter
⅔ cup milk
3 large tart apples
12oz can raspberries, drained
¼ cup granulated sugar
Cream
¼ cup granulated brown sugar

Sieve flour and baking powder into a mixing bowl. Rub in butter excluding 1 tablespoon, and work into a soft dough by adding milk. Knead the dough and roll out onto a floured board. Cut out the scones. Place the scones on a cooky sheet and bake at 450°F for 10-15 minutes. Peel the apples and slice them. Put the apples in a saucepan, and cook in a little water with granulated sugar until soft. Drain the apples and add the raspberries. Cut the scones and sandwich together with butter. Put a circle of scones round the edge of the apple and raspberry mixture. Put some cream in the circle left by the scones. Sprinkle with a little granulated brown sugar and broil until the sugar begins to caramelize. Serve at once.

Snowballs

PREPARATION TIME: 20 minutes

COOKING TIME: 30 minutes then 3 minutes

OVEN: 375°F

6 medium tart apples
⅓ cup soft brown sugar
¾ teaspoon mixed spice
2 eggs
⅓ cup superfine sugar
Candied cherries and angelica
    (optional)

Wash and core the apples. Mix together soft brown sugar and all the spices and fill the center of the apples. Put the apples on a cooky sheet and bake. Beat the egg white until it peaks and fold in the superfine sugar. Coat the apples with meringue and then return to the oven for a few minutes. Decorate with candied cherries and angelica if desired.

Apple Betty

PREPARATION TIME: 30 minutes

COOKING TIME: 30 minutes

OVEN: 350°F

½ cup butter
½ cup fresh white breadcrumbs
½ cup soft brown sugar
½ level teaspoon ground cinnamon
Grated rind and juice of 1 lemon
2lb tart apples, peeled, cored and
    sliced
3 tablespoons water
Ice cream or cream

Melt the butter in a saucepan. Take the pan off the heat and mix in the breadcrumbs. In a bowl mix the sugar, cinnamon and grated lemon rind. Add the apple slices. Butter a 2½ pint pie dish. Sprinkle some of the crumbs in the dish, layer the apple slices with the crumb mixture, ending with the crumb mixture on top. Squeeze the lemon juice and spoon the water over the pudding. Cover the pudding with buttered foil and bake until apples are cooked. The topping should be crisp and golden. Serve with ice cream or cream.

Rainbow Tart

PREPARATION TIME: 15 minutes

COOKING TIME: 35 minutes

OVEN: 375°F

Pastry
2 cups flour
Pinch of salt
¼ cup butter
¼ cup lard
About 3 tablespoons water

Filling
1½ tablespoons strawberry jam
1½ tablespoons blackberry jam
1½ tablespoons bilberry jam
1½ tablespoons lemon curd
1½ tablespoons orange marmalade
1½ tablespoons gooseberry purée
1½ tablespoons mincemeat
Custard

Pastry
Sift flour and salt into a bowl. Cut the butter and lard into pieces and work into the flour with fingers until it looks like breadcrumbs. Stir the water into mixture and mix into a dough. Roll out the pastry on a lightly floured surface. Line a 9 inch pie plate, trim the edges and reserve trimmings for twists.

Filling
Mark the dough and fill in the sections with the jams, curd and mincemeat. Twist the excess dough into spirals and use it to separate the jam sections. Brush the ends with water and press onto the edge to seal. Crimp the edge of pastry case and bake. Remove from the oven and leave to cool for 10 minutes. Serve with pouring custard.

Apple Dumplings with Walnut Sauce

PREPARATION TIME: 30 minutes

COOKING TIME: 35 minutes

OVEN: 400°F

Dumplings
18oz basic pastry
6 large tart apples, cored
9 tablespoons mincemeat
1 egg, lightly beaten

Walnut Sauce
⅓ cup butter
⅓ cup light brown sugar
2½ tablespoons heavy cream
¾ cup chopped walnuts

Divide the dough into 6 portions. Roll out each portion into a round large enough to wrap up one apple. Place the apple in the center of the dough round and fill the cavity (left by removing the core) with mincemeat. Wrap the dough round the apple and moisten the edges with beaten egg. Press together to seal. Place the dumplings on a cooky sheet and brush all over with beaten egg. Bake in preheated, moderately hot oven for 35 minutes or until golden brown. Meanwhile make the sauce.

Walnut Sauce
Melt the butter in a saucepan and stir in all the sugar. When the sugar has dissolved, stir in the cream and walnuts. Heat gently. Serve the dumplings with the sauce; both should be hot.

Facing page: Fruit Cobbler (top), Apple Betty (center) and Yorkshire Apple Tart (bottom).

Winter Fruits

PREPARATION TIME: 15 minutes plus 1 hour soaking

COOKING TIME: 40 minutes

OVEN: 375°F

¾ cup seedless raisins
¾ cup currants
¾ cup white raisins
1 cup chopped mixed candied peel
Finely grated rind and juice of an orange
6 thick slices of toast, crusts removed
About ¼ cup butter
½ cup soft brown sugar
1¼ cups milk
2 eggs, lightly beaten
¼ teaspoon ground cinnamon
Custard

Put all the dried fruit, candied peel, orange rind and juice into a bowl and mix well. Put half the fruit mixture in the bottom of a buttered baking dish. Spread the toast with the butter, then cut it into small squares. Cover the fruit with half the toast and sprinkle with ¼ cup of the soft brown sugar. Repeat the layers again. Mix together the milk, eggs and cinnamon and pour over the layered pudding. Leave the pudding to soak for one hour. Bake in a preheated oven until crisp on top. Serve with thin pouring custard.

Apricot Pudding

PREPARATION TIME: 25 minutes

COOKING TIME: 2 hours

Pastry
1½ cups flour
Pinch of salt
¼ cup sugar
⅓ cup shredded suet
5 tablespoons milk

Filling
1 tart apple
6oz dried apricots, soaked overnight in cold water
⅓ cup seedless raisins
½ teaspoon ground mixed spice
3 tablespoons corn syrup
2-3 tablespoons granulated brown sugar, to finish
Custard or cream

Pastry
Sift the flour and salt into a bowl. Stir in the sugar and suet, add the milk gradually and knead lightly to form a firm dough. Wrap the dough in foil and chill in the fridge.

Filling
Peel and core the apples, then grate into a bowl. Drain the apricots and chop them very finely, then mix in with all the other ingredients for the filling. Roll out the dough on a lightly floured surface. Cut out a small circle large enough to fit the base of a well buttered 3¾ cups pudding mold. Put the dough in the mold. Layer with fruit and a circle of dough (4 layers of dough, 3 layers of filling). Cover the top of the pudding with a circle of buttered wax paper. Cover the mold with foil tied with string. Put the pudding mold in a steamer or in a pan half-filled with boiling water. Cover with a lid and steam. Keep the water level up. Remove the foil and wax disc and let the pudding stand for a few minutes. Turn out carefully on a warmed serving plate and sprinkle with granulated brown sugar. Serve hot with pouring custard or cream.

Rhubarb Tart

PREPARATION TIME: 30 minutes

COOKING TIME: 40 minutes, then another 25 minutes

OVEN: 350°F

Filling
2lb rhubarb, cut into 1 inch pieces.
2⅓ cups sugar
½ cup butter
3 eggs
2 tablespoons white wine
2¼ cups flour
2 teaspoons baking powder

Topping
⅔ cup soured cream
1 teaspoon ground cinnamon
⅓ cup ground almonds
Confectioners' sugar

Put the rhubarb pieces into a bowl, sprinkle with sugar (reserve 10 tablespoons). Cover and allow the rhubarb to draw. Cream the butter and 6 tablespoons of the granulated sugar. Mix together until light and fluffy. Stir in one egg and the wine. Sift in the flour and baking powder. Stir into the other ingredients. Knead the ingredients together to make a smooth dough. Form into a ball, wrap with wax paper and allow to rest for 30 minutes in the fridge. Grease a 10 inch loose-based or spring-clip pie pan. Roll out pastry on a well floured surface. Line pie pan with pastry. Strain the rhubarb, arrange in pastry case and bake.

Topping
Beat the cream and remaining eggs together and stir in the remaining sugar, the cinnamon and ground almonds. Mix thoroughly until smooth. Take the tart out of the oven and pour the topping over the rhubarb. Return to the oven and bake for another 25 minutes. Remove from the oven, turn out and dust with confectioners' sugar, cool before serving.

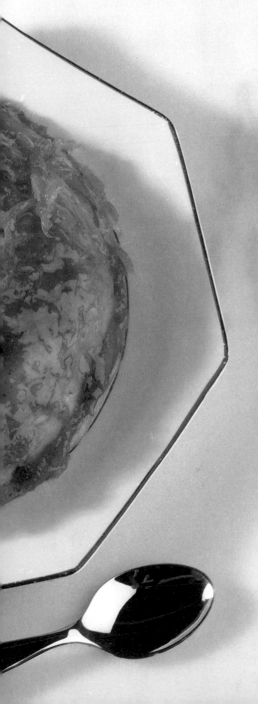

Facing page: Rhubarb Tart (top), Winter Fruits (bottom left) and Apricot Pudding (bottom right).

Carrot Pudding

PREPARATION TIME: 15 minutes

COOKING TIME: 45 minutes

OVEN: 350°F

¼ cup butter
¼ cup sugar
2 eggs, separated
½ cup flour
1 teaspoon ground cinnamon
8oz carrots, peeled and grated
1 tablespoon chopped walnuts
4 tablespoons dry red wine
Grated rind, and juice of 1 lemon
Pinch of salt

Cream the butter with the sugar until the mixture is light and fluffy. Beat in the egg yolks. Sift in the flour and cinnamon, carrots, walnuts, wine, lemon rind, juice and salt. Beat the egg whites until stiff and fold into carrot mixture. Pour into a greased baking dish. Bake in a preheated moderate oven. Serve hot from the dish.

Orange Round

PREPARATION TIME: 30 minutes

COOKING TIME: 15 minutes for pastry 20 minutes for filled flan

OVEN: 350°F

10oz basic pastry
3 oranges, thinly sliced
2 eggs, beaten
½ cup ground almonds
3 tablespoons sugar
3 tablespoons clear honey

Roll out the pastry and line an 8 inch pie dish. Prick the base of the pie. Cut a piece of wax paper, line the pastry and sprinkle with baking beans (or any dried beans, to bake blind). Bake for 10 minutes at 375°F. While the shell is baking, prepare the orange filling. Put the oranges in a saucepan. Add enough water to cover the oranges and simmer for 20 minutes. Cook until the orange peel is soft and drain the water. Beat the egg, almonds and sugar until smooth. Spread the

mixture in the pie shell. Arrange the poached orange slices on top of the mixture. Spoon the clear honey over all the slices. Cook the pie for 20 minutes.

Yuletide Pudding (Round)

PREPARATION TIME: 30 minutes

COOKING TIME: 5 hours plus 3 hours before serving

2¼ cups mixed dried fruit
1¼ cups stoned raisins
⅔ cup chopped mixed peel

1½ cups soft dark brown sugar
⅓ cup almonds, blanched and chopped
¾ cup fresh white breadcrumbs
¾ cup shredded suet
1½ cups flour
½ level teaspoon ground nutmeg
½ level teaspoon ground cinnamon
½ level teaspoon salt
1 carrot, grated
1 tart apple, peeled, cored and grated
Grated rind and juice of 1 lemon
3 tablespoons brandy
1 large egg

Put all ingredients in a large mixing bowl and blend together well. Grease 2 x 2½ pint pudding molds. Put the mixture into the pudding molds, dividing the mixture evenly

between both. Fill the molds, but leave a gap of about 1 inch at the top. Cover both puddings with buttered round of wax paper. Make a foil pudding lid with a pleat and tie securely onto molds. Stand the puddings in pans and add enough water to keep the pans two-thirds full. Cover the pans and boil for 5 hours. Keep the pans topped up with hot water. Remove the molds from water and gently loosen one pudding from its mold, turn it out onto the other pudding. Press the puddings together to make one pudding. Press down on the top pudding. Leave to cool completely, then cover together with wax paper and foil. Before serving boil for three hours. Again make sure the water is topped up. Unwrap carefully and turn out of the bowl.

Pacific Pudding

8oz can pineapple rings
½ cup superfine sugar
½ cup soft margarine
Grated rind of 1 orange
2 eggs, beaten
¾ cup flour, sifted
½ teaspoon baking powder
¼ cup white breadcrumbs
2oz candied cherries, quartered
⅓ cup stoned raisins
1oz angelica
2 tablespoons corn syrup

Drain the pineapple and keep the juice. Cut 3 rings in half and reserve. Chop the remainder coarsely. Cream together the margarine and sugar, add the orange rind and beat in the eggs. Fold in the flour and breadcrumbs. Add the chopped pineapple, cherries, raisins and angelica, and mix well. Butter a 1¾ pint pudding mold. Put the syrup in the bottom and arrange the pineapple rings in a circle. Spoon in the sponge mixture on top and level it. Cover with buttered paper and foil. Put the pudding mold in a saucepan of boiling water two-thirds full. Boil for 1¾ hours. Serve with tangy butter.

This page: Rainbow Tart (top), Carrot Pudding (center) and Apple Dumplings with Walnut Sauce (bottom).

Facing page: Yuletide Pudding (top), Pacific Pudding (center left), Orange Round (center right) and Snowball (bottom).

Special Desserts

Ginger Rum Trifle

PREPARATION TIME: 20 minutes

1½ cups ginger cake, sliced
1½ cups canned pear quarters
9 tablespoons rum
1¾ cups cold thick vanilla sauce
1¼ cups heavy cream
2-3 teaspoons confectioners' sugar
Toasted flaked almonds
Stem ginger cut into strips

Line the bottom of a glass dish with half the ginger cake. Drain the canned pears and mix the rum with the juice. Sprinkle half over the cake. Place the pears on the top of the cake and cover with the remaining slices. Pour over a little more rum mixture. Spoon the sauce over the cake. Whip the cream and gradually add confectioners' sugar until it peaks. Spoon the cream over the sauce and decorate with lightly toasted almond flakes and stem ginger strips.

Lemon Brandy Cream

PREPARATION TIME: 15 minutes

1¼ cups light cream
1¼ cups heavy cream
6 tablespoons soft brown sugar
2 large lemons
6 tablespoons sponge cake
2 tablespoons brandy
2 tablespoons toasted flaked almonds

Mix the light and heavy cream in a small saucepan and add the sugar. Stir over a low heat until the cream begins to bubble. Grate the rind of the lemons and gently stir into the cream. Leave the mixture to cool and crumble the cake crumbs into glasses or serving dish. Stir the brandy into the cream mixture with the juice from both lemons. Pour the mixture into the glasses or dish over the cake crumbs and refrigerate for 30 minutes. Decorate with toasted almond flakes.

Exotic Fruit Salad Basket

PREPARATION TIME: 15 minutes

1 large melon
1 persimmon
3 kiwi fruit, washed
4oz blackberries, washed
6oz raspberries, washed
6oz redcurrants, washed
6oz strawberries, washed
6oz blackcurrants, washed
6oz grapes, red and green

1 mango, peeled and sliced
Strawberry leaves
Use as many fruits in season as are available
Sugar syrup (see Sauces)

Hollow out a melon and reserve the pulp. Slice the persimmon and kiwi fruit, and make melon balls using the reserved melon. Arrange the fruit in the melon basket and spoon over with sugar syrup (see Sauces).

Inset illustration: Lemon Brandy Cream (right), Berry Whip (left).

These pages: Exotic Fruit Salad (top left), Cranberry Fool (top right) and Ginger Rum Trifle (bottom).

Cranberry Fool, Chilled

PREPARATION TIME: 30 minutes

1lb cranberries
10 tablespoons sugar
2 tablespoons lemon juice
⅔ cup carton soured cream

Bring the cranberries to the boil in 1¾ cups water in a saucepan, then simmer for about 15 minutes. Cool and stir in the sugar until dissolved. Purée the mixture until most of it is smooth by rubbing it through a sieve to remove the cranberry skins. Make sure the mixture is cool, stir in the lemon juice, cover and chill. Spoon into serving dish and serve with sour cream.

Berry Whip

PREPARATION TIME: 15 minutes

3 egg whites
A few grains of salt
¾ cup confectioners' sugar
½lb blackberries
Sponge fingers

In a deep bowl beat the egg whites. Add the sugar and salt and beat until very stiff. Fold in the berries. Spoon into glasses and chill. Serve with sponge fingers.

Cremets

PREPARATION TIME: 10 minutes

1½ cups curd cheese
2 tablespoons vanilla sugar or superfine sugar with a few drops of vanilla essence
1¼ cups heavy cream

Beat the curd cheese until smooth. Add the sugar and gradually beat in the cream. Pile into a bowl and chill.

Almond Galette

PREPARATION TIME: 1 hour
COOKING TIME: 10 minutes for each batch of rounds
OVEN: 375°F

1½ cups butter
2 cups superfine sugar
2 eggs
2¾ cups all-purpose flour
2 tablespoons ground almonds
3¾ cups heavy cream, whipped
Confectioners' sugar
Heavy cream
Whole almonds

Cut out 9 inch circles of non-stick baking paper. Cream the sugar and butter together and beat in the eggs. Fold in the sifted flour and ground almonds. Divide the mixture into 12 and using a large palette knife coat the individual paper rounds with the mixture. Work from the center outwards with smooth strokes. Wet a cooky sheet and bake the rounds. Leave until cool and carefully peel off the paper. When all the rounds are cooked use them to form layers, spreading each one with whipped cream. Reserve ⅔ cup of cream for

decoration. Dust the top with confectioners' sugar and decorate with almonds and cream.

Blackberry, Raisin and Walnut Jelly

PREPARATION TIME: 10 minutes
Note: In order that the fruit should be plump, soak overnight.

½ cup seedless raisins
2 tablespoons rum
1 packet blackberry jelly
1¼ cups port
1lb frozen blackberries (keep frozen)
6 walnuts halved
Cream
Flowers

Soak the raisins in the rum for a few hours, preferably overnight. Dissolve the jelly in 1¼ cups of boiling water. Add the port and cool, making sure the jelly does not set. Put the fruit and nuts in individual glasses or a mold, making sure they are quite full. Spoon over the jelly and leave to set. Decorate with flowers and/or cream.

French Plum Pudding

PREPARATION TIME: 20 minutes
COOKING TIME: 40 minutes
OVEN: 400°F

¾ cup all-purpose flour
¾ cup butter
6 tablespoons superfine sugar
¼ cup ground almonds
1 egg yolk
1 tablespoon cold water
1½lb plums, halved and stoned

Sift the flour into a mixing bowl. Cut in two-thirds of the butter and 2 tablespoons of the sugar. Add the ground almonds and mix into a firm dough with the egg yolk and water. Chill. Melt the reserved butter in a 9 inch round ovenproof dish. Add the remaining sugar until caramelized. Remove from heat. Arrange the plums, skin side down, in the ovenproof dish. On a lightly floured surface roll out the dough into a round slightly bigger than the dish. Place the dough on top of the plums and gently press down, tucking in the edges as you go. Bake in the oven until golden. To serve, turn out onto a serving dish. Serve instantly.

Chocolate Meringues

PREPARATION TIME: 40 minutes
COOKING TIME: 2 hours
(leave the meringues to cool for as long as necessary)
OVEN: 250°F

4 egg whites
1 cup superfine sugar
¼ cup hazelnuts, finely ground
1¼ cups heavy cream
1 tablespoon cocoa powder
Chocolate curls

Beat the egg whites until stiff. Gently whisk in the sugar a little at a time and fold in the hazelnuts with a metal spoon. Spoon out rounds of meringue onto a cooky sheet lined with non-stick wax paper. Bake until well dried out. Cool on wire racks. Whip the cream until stiff and fold in the cocoa powder. Use the cream to sandwich the meringues and decorate with chocolate shavings or curls.

Coconut Cup

PREPARATION TIME: 35 minutes

3 coconuts sawed in half
3 scoops soft-scoop vanilla ice cream per half coconut
3 tablespoons dark rum
1lb dried mixed fruit

Soak fruit in rum overnight. Saw coconuts in half and remove the flesh. Grate half the flesh, and incorporate in the ice cream along with the fruit, reserving some of the fruit for decoration. Fill coconut halves with mixture and place in freezer until firm. To serve, top with remaining fruit and grated coconut.

This page: Cremet (left), Almond Galette (right).

Facing page: Blackberry, Raisin and Walnut Jelly (top right), French Plum Pudding (center left) and Chocolate Meringues (bottom).

Blackberry Ice Cream Dessert

PREPARATION TIME: 20 minutes plus freezing time

6 tablespoons sugar
1½ tablespoons Curaçao
1⅓ cups blackberry purée
¾ cup low-fat plain yogurt
Generous pinch of cinnamon
⅔ cup heavy cream, whipped
⅔ cup water

Boil the sugar with the water for a minute and add the Curaçao. Stir in the blackberry purée (rub the fruit through a nylon sieve). Stir in the yogurt and cinnamon, and lastly fold in the whipped cream. Freeze until creamy and serve.

Kiwi Cheesecake

PREPARATION TIME: 45 minutes
COOKING TIME: 20 minutes
OVEN: 350°F

Base
¼ cup soft butter
¼ cup superfine sugar
1 egg
10 tablespoons all-purpose flour
½ teaspoon baking powder
Finely grated rind of ½ medium
  orange

Filling
¾ cup cream cheese
¼ cup superfine sugar
3 eggs, separated
Juice of 1 medium orange
Finely grated rind of ½ medium
  orange
½oz gelatin
4 tablespoons cold water
⅔ cup natural yogurt
⅔ cup heavy cream

To decorate
⅔ cup heavy cream
3 kiwi fruit, peeled and sliced
Nuts

Base
Grease and line the base and sides of an 8 inch loose bottom cake pan with wax paper. Note: The paper should come over the top of the pan. In a mixing bowl add the butter, egg and superfine sugar and cream the mixture until fluffy. Sieve the flour and baking powder into the bowl and beat. Add the

orange rind. Use either a wooden spoon or electric beater for two or one minute respectively. Spoon the mixture into the cake pan and cook for 20 minutes, 350°F. Leave in pan when cooked and allow to cool.

Filling
While the base is cooking, beat the sugar with cream cheese and add the egg yolks, orange juice and rind. Beat until very smooth. In a heatproof basin put the cold water and sprinkle in the gelatin, leaving it to stand for 10 minutes until soft. Stand the basin in a pan of simmering water until gelatin dissolves. Stir constantly. Leave to cool but not set. Pour the gelatin in a constant stream into the cheese mixture and stir. Beat in the yogurt. Whip the cream and fold carefully into the mixture using a metal spoon. Beat the egg whites in a clean bowl until stiff and fold into cheese mixture. Pour the cheese mixture over the base and smooth

the top. Leave to set in the fridge for several hours.

To decorate
Remove from the pan and carefully peel off the paper, serve decorated with cream, kiwi fruit and nuts (an alternative could be orange segments). Serve chilled.

Poached Minty Pears

PREPARATION TIME: 40 minutes plus chilling

6 large pears, peeled
6 tablespoons sugar
Fresh mint leaves
6 tablespoons clear honey
3 tablespoons Creme de Menthe
  liqueur

Put the pears in a saucepan. Stand upright and pour water over.

Cover all the pears. Boil and then simmer for 30 minutes. Pour off half the water and sprinkle over with sugar. Add the fresh mint and simmer for 10 minutes. Transfer the pears to a bowl. Reserve ⅔ cup water from the pan and stir in the honey and liqueur. Pour this mixture over the pears and allow it to cool. Cover the pears and chill for 2 hours. Stand each pear on an individual serving dish and spoon over the mint sauce.

This page: Blackberry Ice-Cream Dessert (top), Coconut Cups (bottom).

Facing page: Kiwi Cheesecake (top), Poached Minty Pear (bottom).

Coffee Truffles

PREPARATION TIME: 10 minutes

1 cup cake crumbs
2 tablespoons ground almonds
¼ teaspoon coffee powder
Heaped tablespoon apricot jam, melted
2-3 tablespoons coffee liqueur
2oz chocolate vermicelli

Put the crumbs and ground almonds into a bowl. Mix in the jam and coffee liqueur and mix together to form a stiff paste. Shape into small balls and roll in chocolate vermicelli.

Crystal Fruits

1 egg white
8oz bunch of grapes
2 large red apples
2 large pears
½ cup plums
Any other soft fruit in season

Beat the egg white well and brush onto the fruit. Leave for a few minutes but not until dry. Dip the fruit into superfine sugar and place on wax paper until dry. Arrange in fruit bowl or stand.

Apricot Mountain

PREPARATION TIME: 20 minutes

COOKING TIME: 4 minutes or until meringue is brown

OVEN: 450°F

About ¾lb canned apricot halves
4-6 tablespoons Marsala or sweet sherry
3 egg whites
½ cup superfine sugar
8 inch sponge tart case
1¾ cups vanilla ice cream

Strain the apricots and sprinkle them with the sherry. Beat the egg whites until stiff and fold in the sugar. Beat again until the meringue peaks. Stand the tart case on a heatproof dish and sprinkle with a little more sherry. Pile the apricots into the tart case. Cover the apricots with a mountain shape of ice cream. Using the meringue mixture, quickly cover the ice cream and the sponge base. Bake immediately until the meringue is light brown. Serve from the oven.

For a very special effect bury half an egg shell at the top of the mountain before baking the meringue. As you serve fill it with warmed brandy, ignite and serve flaming.

Petits Fours

PREPARATION TIME: 40 minutes
OVEN: 400°F

Sponge
3 eggs
½ cup superfine sugar
¾ cup all-purpose flour
1 tablespoon hot water

Topping
Fruits in season
Apricot jam to glaze

Sponge
Beat eggs and sugar until thick and creamy. Sift in flour and fold in with the hot water. Place mixture in a greased and floured jelly roll pan. Bake for 8 to 10 minutes until cake springs back when pressed. Turn out and cool. Cut shapes out of the sponge using pastry cutters.

Topping
Place sponge shapes on a wire rack and top with attractively arranged fruit. Melt apricot jam on low heat and spoon over shapes to glaze. When surplus has dripped off and jam has set remove and place on serving plate.

Chocolate Leaf, Filled with Orange Mousse

PREPARATION TIME: 1 hour
plus chilling

For the Leaf
6oz semi-sweet chocolate
1 cabbage leaf (with veins)

Mousse
3 whole eggs plus 2 yolks
¼ cup superfine sugar
Juice of ½ lemon
1½ tablespoons powdered gelatin
⅔ cup heavy cream
⅔ cup freshly squeezed orange juice
Finely grated rind of 2 oranges

Leaf
Put the chocolate in a basin over simmering water and stir until smooth. With a pastry brush, paint the chocolate over a well-veined cabbage leaf and leave to cool and harden. Repeat the process until there is a thick build up of chocolate on the leaf. When hard the cabbage leaf can be easily removed.

Mousse
Put the eggs and yolks in a basin with the sugar. Beat until pale and frothy. This can be done over a saucepan of simmering water, but make sure that the basin doesn't touch the water. Beat until thick. Remove from the heat and beat until cold. Put the lemon juice and a little water into a small saucepan and sprinkle in the gelatin and leave it to soak for a few minutes. Whip the cream and stir it into the egg mixture, gradually adding the orange juice and grated rind. Gently heat the gelatin until clear and stir it quickly into the mixture. Fill the serving dish and refrigerate until set. This mousse can either be served with one leaf or several small leaves to go with each portion of mousse.

Crystal Fruits (left), Coffee Truffles (bottom left) and Petits Fours (bottom right).

Fruit Salad with Mango Purée

PREPARATION TIME: 20 minutes plus 1 hour chilling in the refrigerator

3 peaches
3 tamarillos (tree tomatoes)
3 kiwi fruit
1½ tablespoons lemon juice
3 tablespoons sugar syrup

Mango Purée
2 well-ripened mangoes weighing
    about 12oz
Juice of ½ a lime, or lemon
3 teaspoons honey
5oz redcurrants
Strawberry leaves for decoration

Blanch the peaches briefly and peel. Halve and remove stones and cut into delicate wedges. Peel and slice the tamarillos, nectarines and kiwi fruit, arrange in serving dish and scatter over with redcurrants. Pour over the lemon juice mixed with sugar syrup. Leave the fruits to stand in syrup for 1 hour in a cool place.

Mango Purée
Either liquidize or rub through a wire sieve the flesh of the mangoes and mix with the lime juice. Mix in the honey and pour the mixture over the fruit. Decorate with strawberry leaves.

Pineapple Malibu

PREPARATION TIME: 30 minutes

1 medium ripe pineapple
2 cups heavy cream
6 tablespoons macaroons, roughly
    crushed
3 tablespoons coconut liqueur

Cut the pineapple a few inches below the top. Scoop out as much of the fruit as possible, discarding the core if hard. Chop the fruit into bite-size pieces. Whip two-thirds of the cream until it begins to stiffen and fold in the macaroons, having first soaked them in the coconut liqueur. In another bowl whip up the remaining cream and fold into the coconut cream. Spoon alternate spoonfuls of diced pineapple and cream mixture into the hollowed pineapple and chill. Serve straight from the fridge.

Chocolate Ginger Tart

PREPARATION TIME: 30 minutes

4oz semi-sweet chocolate
1¼ cups milk
½ cup superfine sugar
3 tablespoons flour
½ cup butter
2 egg yolks
6oz ginger nut cookies
Whipped cream
4oz stem ginger cut into thin slices

Melt the chocolate in the milk in a saucepan, stirring constantly. Remove pan from heat. Mix the superfine sugar, flour and ¼ cup butter into the chocolate milk and stir in the egg yolks. Put on a low heat and slowly bring to the boil. Simmer for 5 minutes until the mixture begins to thicken, stir until smooth. Remove from heat and cool. While the filling is cooling, melt the remaining ¼ cup of butter and crush the ginger nut cookies. Mix the cookies with the melted butter and press in a greased pie pan. When the filling is cool, pour onto the ginger nut base. Chill and decorate with whipped cream and sprinkle with stemmed ginger cut into thin slices (an alternative decoration is chocolate vermicelli).

Coffee Charlotte

PREPARATION TIME: 1½ hours
COOKING TIME: 12 minutes
OVEN: 475°F

Sponge
4 egg yolks
¼ cup sugar
Generous pinch of salt
3 egg whites
5 tablespoons flour mixed with 2
    teaspoons coffee powder
¾ cup apricot jam
3 tablespoons brandy
2 tablespoons cornstarch

set, carefully fold in the cream and fill the sponge-lined mold. Stir in the marinated apricot and cover the top of the mold with slices from the sponge roll. Let the charlotte set for three hours in the refrigerator and turn onto a serving dish. Brush with the apricot glaze.

Orange Campari Mousse

PREPARATION TIME: 45 minutes
plus chilling

1 teaspoon powdered gelatin
2 medium oranges, washed and dried
7 tablespoons superfine sugar
2 eggs, separated
3 tablespoons Campari
⅔ cup heavy cream
1 tablespoon cold milk
Red grapes

Add gelatin to two tablespoons of water in a saucepan. Leave to one side. Grate peel of 1 orange. Squeeze oranges and if necessary make up juice to ¾ cup with water. Melt gelatin and water over a low heat. Stir in orange juice. Pour mixture into a bowl, beat in sugar, egg yolks, Campari and orange peel. Place in fridge until the mixture begins to thicken and set. In one bowl beat egg whites until stiff. In another beat milk and cream together until thick. Gradually mix egg whites and cream alternately into the orange mixture until totally incorporated. Pour into a bowl and place in refrigerator until firm and set. Serve in glasses decorated with sliced red grapes.

Charlotte
6 apricot halves
1 tablespoon vanilla sugar
1 tablespoon brandy
4 egg yolks
½ cup sugar
Plus 1 tablespoon sugar
1 cup milk
½ vanilla pod
½oz powdered gelatin
1 cup heavy cream
⅓ cup apricot glaze (warmed apricot jam)

Sponge
Beat the egg yolks with a spoonful of sugar and the salt. Beat the egg whites and fold the egg yolk mixture into the meringue. Sift together the cornstarch and flour and stir them in. Line a jelly roll pan with non-stick wax paper. Spread the sponge mixture evenly in the jelly roll pan using a spatula. Bake until golden. Turn it out at once onto a clean, damp cloth and peel off the paper. Blend the jam with the brandy and spread the sponge cake with it. Roll it up. Let it cool and cut into thin slices ¼ inch thick. Line the mold with the slices as close together as possible.

Charlotte
Place the apricot halves in a dish and sprinkle them with vanilla sugar. Pour over the brandy. Leave them to marinate in the refrigerator for half an hour. Cream the egg yolks and sugar together in a mixing bowl and put the milk in a small saucepan with the vanilla pod. Heat the milk and bring to the boil and pour into the egg yolks. Return the sauce mixture to the saucepan and stir until it is thick enough to coat the spoon. Remove from heat. Dissolve the gelatin in warm water and stir in the tablespoon of brandy. Add to the sauce mixture and stir well. Cool the sauce. Meanwhile stiffly whip the cream, adding the remaining sugar. When the sauce begins to

Facing page: Apricot Mountain (left), Orange Campari Mousse (right).

This page: Chocolate Leaf, Filled with Orange Mousse (top), Chocolate Ginger Tart (center left) and Fruit Salad with Mango Purée (bottom right).

Chestnut Parfait

PREPARATION TIME: 40 minutes
plus freezing

4 egg yolks
10 tablespoons sugar
⅔ cup milk, warmed and flavored
  with a vanilla pod
14 tablespoons unsweetened chestnut
  purée
2 tablespoons dark rum
2 egg whites
¼ cup sugar
2 cups heavy cream
Chocolate leaves
A few cranberries
Whipped cream

Beat the egg yolks with the sugar and add the warmed milk flavored with the vanilla pod and cook until thickened, stirring gently. The mixture should coat the spoon. Transfer to a mixing bowl. Add the chestnut purée and rum while the mixture is still lukewarm. Chill well. Whip the egg whites with the sugar until very stiff. Beat the cream until it peaks. Fold the egg white into the chestnut cream and carefully fold in the whipped cream. Pour into a 6 cup mold and freeze for 4 hours. Decorate with small rounds of sweetened chestnut purée dusted with chocolate powder or melted chocolate sauce.

Strawberry Shortcake

PREPARATION TIME: 1 hour
COOKING TIME: 25 minutes
OVEN: 425°F

Shortcake
2 cups all-purpose flour
Pinch of salt
4 teaspoons baking powder
6 tablespoons butter
1 large egg
3 tablespoons superfine sugar
3 tablespoons milk
1 tablespoon melted butter

Filling
2 egg yolks
2 drops vanilla essence
1¼ cups milk
2 tablespoons sugar
⅔ cup heavy cream
1lb fresh or thawed, frozen
  strawberries
8 toasted almonds

Shortcake
Sift the flour, salt and baking powder into a bowl. With a knife, mix in the butter. Beat in the egg, sugar and milk and pour into the center of the dry ingredients. Mix into a dough. On a lightly floured surface knead gently and divide into two. Brush an 8 inch cake pan with melted butter and shape half the dough into a circle to fit. Place the second circle on top and bake until risen and golden brown. Cool and separate the two halves.

Filling
Make up the vanilla sauce. Heat the milk in a saucepan with the sugar and vanilla essence. Beat the yolks in a bowl and pour on the hot milk. Blend and return to the pan. Stir over a gentle heat until the sauce thickens enough to coat the back of a wooden spoon. Cover and leave to cool. Whisk the cream until just stiff. Fold the cream into the cooled sauce, reserving two tablespoons for decoration. Reserving 8 whole strawberries and one-third of the sauce mixture, halve the remaining strawberries and mix into the sauce. Spread the strawberry sauce on the bottom layer of the shortbread and sandwich with the top layer. Spread the top with the reserved sauce mixture and decorate with whole strawberries and almonds.

Green Devils

PREPARATION TIME: 20 minutes
plus chilling

1½lb dessert gooseberries
¾ cup superfine sugar
2½ cups water
3 tablespoons grenadine
Juice ½ lemon
1 level tablespoon cornstarch
Cream

Rinse and top and tail the gooseberries. Put the superfine sugar in a small saucepan and dissolve it in the water. Simmer and bring to the boil. Take off heat and stir in the grenadine, lemon juice and gooseberries and bring back to simmer. Cook very gently for five minutes until the fruit is tender. Remove from heat. Lift out the fruit and put into the serving dish. Mix the cornstarch with a little water to make a thin paste. Stir into the fruit juice till it begins to thicken. Stir all the time. When the syrup is clear, pour over the fruit. Chill, preferably overnight, and serve with thick pouring cream.

Facing page: Pineapple Malibu (top), Coffee Charlotte (center right) and Chestnut Parfait (bottom).

This page: Green Devils (top), Strawberry Shortcake (bottom).

QuickDesserts

Zabaglione

PREPARATION TIME: 5 minutes

COOKING TIME: 10 minutes

4 egg yolks
4 tablespoons sugar
4 tablespoons Marsala wine

Put all the ingredients into a large heatproof bowl. Beat with a wire whisk until light and frothy. Stand the bowl in a pan of water over a low heat and continue to beat. The mixture will froth and is now ready to serve. Pour into heatproof glasses and serve immediately with the sponge fingers. An instant Italian dessert. Note: Do not overheat or the mixture will curdle and not become frothy.

Raspberry Brioches

PREPARATION TIME: 15 minutes

12 small brioches (use either fresh or
    frozen brioches, or choux buns as
    illustrated).
¼ cup sugar
1 tablespoon lemon juice
2 tablespoons honey
⅔ cup water
1 teaspoon raspberry liqueur
1lb fresh raspberries
2 tablespoons toasted, flaked
    almonds

Let the sugar, lemon juice, honey and water boil for three minutes. Add the raspberry liqueur. Using some of the syrup, soak the brioches. Fill with the raspberries. Sprinkle over the rest of the syrup and add the flaked almonds. Serve.

This page: Poor Knights of Windsor (top left), Zabaglione (top right) and Coffee Liqueur Crêpes (bottom).

Facing page: Lemon Syllabub (top), Hot Fruit Brioches (center) and Raspberry Brioches (bottom).

Hot Fruit Brioches

PREPARATION TIME: 20 minutes

12 small brioches
⅓ cup sugar
⅔ cup water
10oz apricots, peeled and halved
6oz fresh blackberries
3 tablespoons brandy

Sabayon Sauce
6 egg yolks
1 cup sugar
1 cup very dry white wine

Heat the sugar and water in a saucepan. Add the apricots and poach until glossy. Meanwhile make up the sabayon sauce and reserve. Add the blackberries and brandy, leave for 4 minutes and reserve them. Cut the tops off the brioches and hollow them. Fill the hollowed brioches with the poached apricots and saturate the top with remaining syrup. Pour over sabayon sauce and put the lid on. A last minute alternative. They are delicious with hot stewed fruit, and the sabayon sauce adds a dash of extravagance.

Sabayon Sauce
Cream the egg yolks and sugar together. Place the bowl over warm water and add the wine. Stir continuously.

Poor Knights of Windsor

PREPARATION TIME and COOKING TIME:
15 minutes inclusive

1 egg
1 tablespoon of milk
2 tablespoons sugar
6 small slices of fruit or plain bread, crusts removed
¼ cup butter
1 teaspoon ground cinnamon

To decorate
15oz can apricot halves in juice (drained)
Whipped cream
1 tablespoon toasted almonds

Beat the egg and mix with sugar and milk. Dip the bread into this mixture and fry. Sprinkle bread with ground cinnamon and decorate with apricot halves, whipped cream and toasted almonds. Serve hot.

Coffee Liqueur Crêpes

PREPARATION TIME: 35 minutes

Crêpes
1 cup flour
Pinch of salt
1 teaspoon sugar
1 cup cold milk
1 egg
4 tablespoons cold, strong black coffee
1 teaspoon vegetable oil
Oil for frying

Sauce
1 tablespoon butter
Grated rind and juice of ½ a lemon
2 tablespoons coffee liqueur

Crêpes
Sift the flour, salt and sugar into a bowl. Add the milk, egg, coffee and oil and beat until smooth. Lightly oil a frying pan and fry the crêpes until golden brown. Toss and cook on the other side. Keep the crêpes warm.

Sauce
Melt the butter in a large frying pan. Arrange the crêpes folded in the pan. Add the lemon rind and juice and coffee liqueur. Heat gently until hot. Serve immediately.

Syllabub

PREPARATION TIME: 10 minutes plus overnight soaking

Thinly pared rind of 1 lemon
6 tablespoons of lemon juice
9 tablespoons sweet white wine or sherry
3 tablespoons brandy
⅓ cup sugar
1¾ cups heavy cream
Grated nutmeg

Put the lemon rind and juice, brandy and wine or sherry in a bowl. Leave overnight. Remove the lemon rind and stir in the sugar. Gradually stir in the cream until it peaks. This will require beating. Spoon into glasses and sprinkle with grated nutmeg.

Caramel Oranges

PREPARATION TIME: 15 minutes

6 oranges (large and juicy)
¾ cup sugar
1¾ cups water

Peel the oranges. Put the sugar and water in a heavy saucepan. Boil the mixture until it begins to caramelize. Place the oranges in a presentation dish and pour over the liquid caramel. Serve immediately.

Blackberry Fluff

PREPARATION TIME: 10 minutes

1lb blackberries, drained
1¼ cups heavy cream
1 egg white
¼ cup sugar
Pieces of angelica to decorate
Ladyfinger confections

Sieve the blackberries. Beat the cream until thick and stir into the blackberry purée. Beat the egg white, adding the sugar slowly, until the mixture is stiff. Fold the egg white into the blackberry cream. Spoon into individual serving glasses and serve with ladyfinger confections. A quick and luscious dessert. Make it in advance but in individual glasses. Store in the refrigerator and serve chilled.

Spiced Pears

PREPARATION TIME: 20 minutes

1½lb can of pear halves
1½ cups red wine
3 teaspoons ground cinnamon
3oz stem ginger, chopped

Drain the pears, saving ⅔ cup of the juice. Put the pears in the wine with the juice and cinnamon. Boil for 10 minutes and reduce the heat. Simmer for ten minutes. Add the chopped ginger and leave to cool. Serve chilled.

Cherries Jubilee

PREPARATION TIME: 10 minutes

1½lb canned black cherries
1½ tablespoons grated lemon rind
3 tablespoons cornstarch
6 tablespoons brandy
Vanilla ice cream

Drain the cherries, reserving the juice. Put all except one tablespoon of juice into a saucepan, add the lemon rind and bring to the boil. Simmer for 2 minutes and strain the juice. Return the juice to the saucepan and add the cherries. In the reserved tablespoon of juice, dissolve the cornstarch. Add this to the saucepan and stir constantly until thick. Warm the brandy and set it alight. Pour it as it flames into the cherry mixture and stir until the flames die down. Serve immediately with ice cream.

Redcurrant and Blackcurrant Compote

PREPARATION TIME: 10 minutes plus chilling

1½lb redcurrants or 12oz each of redcurrants and blackcurrants)
1¼ cups sugar
1 tablespoon water
2 tablespoons gin or brandy
Whipped cream
Sponge fingers

Put the fruit, sugar and water into a saucepan. Shake gently over the heat until sugar has dissolved. Remove from heat and stir in the gin or brandy. Cool. Spoon the compote into serving dishes. Chill for three hours before serving. Serve with the cream and sponge fingers.

Tarte Aux Fruits

PREPARATION TIME: 15 minutes

1 pie shell or sponge shell
1lb grapes, black and green (or 1lb fresh fruit or canned or bottled fruit)
2½ cups vanilla sauce (optional)

Glaze
1¼ cups juice from the fruit after poaching
OR
drained syrup from can
OR
1 heaped tablespoon apricot jam
OR
sugar syrup

Facing page: Caramel Oranges (top), Blackberry Fluff (center left) and Cherries in Wine (bottom).

second to warm the brandy through. Ignite, and let the flames die naturally. Serve at once. Serve hot with light cream.

Raspberry Jelly Mold

PREPARATION TIME: 8-10 minutes
plus setting

1 packet raspberry jelly
1¼ cups milk
⅔ cup water
8oz fresh or thawed, frozen
 raspberries
⅔ cup water to melt jelly
Cream

Put the jelly into a saucepan with ⅔ cup water and melt slowly. Stand until the jelly is tepid, then slowly stir in 1¼ cups of milk and ⅔ cup of water. Wet the jelly mold and fill with the fruit. Pour in the jelly and leave until set. To serve, decorate with any fruit, and cream.

Simple Trifles

PREPARATION TIME: 15 minutes

6 sponge fingers (2in x 3½ ins
 approx.)
3 tablespoons Cointreau or orange
 liqueur
3 oranges
4 tablespoons lemon curd
3 egg whites
6 lemon twists

Break sponge fingers into pieces and place in 6 individual dishes. Sprinkle each one with half a tablespoon of Cointreau. Peel the oranges. Chop them and remove all pith. Divide equally between the portions. Place the lemon curd in a bowl. Beat the egg whites until stiff and fold them into the lemon curd. Spoon this mixture over each serving and decorate with twists of lemon. Chill and serve.

Halve and stone the grapes. Place them cut side down in alternate rings around a pie shell. Glaze with one heaped tablespoon of warmed apricot jam, poured and brushed over the fruit. Alternatively, spread the base of the tart with 2½ cups of made vanilla sauce before covering with fruit. Glaze with either apricot jam or sugar syrup.

Cherries in Wine

PREPARATION TIME: 5 minutes
COOKING TIME: 10 minutes

1lb cherries, stoned
½ teaspoon ground cinnamon
4 tablespoons sugar
1¼ cups light red wine
4 tablespoons redcurrant jelly
2 teaspoons cornstarch

Put the cherries, cinnamon, sugar and most of the wine into a heavy saucepan. Boil slowly. Mix the redcurrant jelly and cornstarch with the rest of the wine and form into a paste before stirring into the saucepan. Simmer for three minutes, then remove from heat. Leave covered for five minutes. Serve cold.

Brandy Bananas

PREPARATION TIME: 10 minutes

6 tablespoons butter
3 tablespoons soft brown sugar
3 tablespoons lemon juice
6 bananas
3 tablespoons brandy
Light cream

Put the butter, sugar and lemon juice in a frying pan. Add the bananas and fry gently, making sure they are coated with the mixture. Add the brandy and cook for a

This page: Brandy Bananas (top left), Cherries Jubilee (center right) and Spiced Pears (bottom).

Facing page: Simple Trifle (top left), Tarte Aux Fruits (top right), Redcurrant and Blackcurrant Compote (far right) and Raspberry Jelly Mold (bottom).

Stuffed Baked Peaches

PREPARATION TIME: 15 minutes

COOKING TIME: 30 minutes

OVEN: 350°F

6 large peaches, peeled, halved and
    stoned
3oz macaroons, crushed
4 tablespoons ground almonds
1 teaspoon finely grated orange rind
2 egg yolks
3 tablespoons butter, cut into small
    pieces
1 cup sweet white wine

Put the peaches on a baking dish,
cut side up. In a small mixing bowl
put the macaroons, almonds,
orange rind and egg yolks. Mix
together and use to fill the peaches.
Put a knob of butter on top of each
peach. Pour the wine into the
baking dish and bake. Serve warm.

Fruit Salad with Cottage Cheese

PREPARATION TIME: 20 minutes

3oz cranberries
3oz raspberries
4 tablespoons orange juice
5 tablespoons granulated sugar
2 tablespoons brandy
1 ogen melon
3 kiwi fruit
3 tablespoons confectioners' sugar
1 cup cottage cheese

Raspberry Sauce
7oz raspberries
6 tablespoons sugar
⅓ cup red wine
Small piece of lemon rind
Walnut pieces to decorate

Boil the cranberries, raspberries
and orange juice with the
granulated sugar for five minutes.
Strain the mixture through a sieve.
Stir in the brandy and cool. Peel
and slice the melon and kiwi fruit.
Arrange the fruit on individual
plates. Stir the confectioners' sugar
into the cottage cheese and place a
little on top of each plateful of fruit.
Chill. Decorate using any of the
fruit contained in the sauce.

Raspberry Sauce
Purée the raspberries. Boil for 5
minutes adding the sugar and wine
and lemon rind. Continue to boil
for three minutes. Serve hot or
cold.

Baked Orange Rhubarb

PREPARATION TIME: 10 minutes

COOKING TIME: 45 minutes

OVEN: 325°F

2lb rhubarb, cut into 1 inch pieces
1 finely grated rind of, and juice of
    one orange
6 tablespoons clear honey

Place the rhubarb in a baking dish
and sprinkle over the orange rind,
juice and honey. Cover and bake in
a moderate oven. Serve.

Plums Baked in Port

PREPARATION TIME: 5 minutes

COOKING TIME: 45 minutes

OVEN: 300°F

2lb plums, halved and stoned
½ cup brown sugar
⅔ cup port

Place the plums in a baking dish.
Sprinkle over the sugar and port.
Cover them and bake in a cool
oven until the plums are tender.
Serve warm or lightly chilled.

Pêches Carmen

PREPARATION TIME: 10 minutes

8 ripe peaches
1½lb raspberries
2 tablespoons kirsch
½ cup confectioners' sugar

Slice the peaches into a serving
dish. Add the raspberries and
kirsch. Leave to stand for an hour
in a cool place. Spoon into
individual dishes and sprinkle with
confectioners' sugar. Chill and
serve with cream.

Facing page: Highland Cream and Ginger Snaps (top), Stuffed Baked Peaches (center) and Fruit Salad with Cottage Cheese (bottom).

This page: (left picture) Pêches Carmen (top), Stuffed Oranges (center) and Plums in Port (bottom). (Right picture) Sour Cream Peaches (top), Ginger Roll (center) and Baked Orange Rhubarb (bottom).

Sour Cream Peaches

PREPARATION TIME: 10 minutes

COOKING TIME: 10 minutes

6 large peaches, peeled, sliced and
  stoned
3 tablespoons brown sugar
½ teaspoon ground cinnamon
1¼ cups sour cream
6 tablespoons granulated sugar

Divide the peach slices between 6 flameproof serving dishes. Mix together the brown sugar and cinnamon. Sprinkle this over the peaches. Spoon the sour cream over the top. Sprinkle a tablespoon of sugar over each portion. Broil quickly until the sugar melts and caramelizes.

Ginger Roll

PREPARATION TIME: This dish should be started the night before required, to allow the ginger cookies to absorb the rum.

36 ginger cookies
6 tablespoons rum
2½ cups heavy cream
2 teaspoons ground ginger
2 teaspoons soft brown sugar
2 tablespoons ginger syrup (from stem
  ginger)
Stem ginger slices

Put the cookies in a flat dish and sprinkle with rum. When the rum has been completely absorbed, beat the cream with the ground ginger and sugar and add the ginger syrup. Use some of the cream to sandwich together the cookies.

Cover with the remaining cream and decorate with stem ginger slices. Serve.

Stuffed Oranges

PREPARATION TIME: 15 minutes

3 large oranges
2 dessert apples, peeled, cored and
  chopped
1½ tablespoons raisins
1½ tablespoons dates, chopped
1½ tablespoons nuts, toasted and
  chopped
1½ tablespoons soft brown sugar
¾ cup heavy cream
2 teaspoons confectioners' sugar
Orange twists

Halve the oranges and scoop out the flesh, keeping the shells intact. Chop the flesh, discarding all the pith, and put it in a bowl. Add to the orange flesh the brown sugar, apple, raisins, dates and nuts. Mix well. Scoop the mixture back into the orange halves. Whip the cream with the confectioners' sugar until it forms soft peaks. Spoon this cream on top of the orange mixture. Chill and serve. Decorate with twists of orange.

Highland Cream Served with Ginger Snaps

PREPARATION TIME: 15 minutes

4 tablespoons ginger marmalade
1½ cups heavy cream
4 tablespoons sugar
3 tablespoons whisky
3 tablespoons lemon juice
3 egg whites
Soft brown sugar
1 packet ginger cookies

Divide the marmalade between serving dishes. Whip the cream, adding the caster sugar gradually. Fold in the whisky and lemon juice. Beat the egg whites and fold into the cream. With a spoon, put a little of the cream mixture over the marmalade. Decorate with brown sugar and ginger cookies.

Orange Tart

PREPARATION TIME: 30 minutes
COOKING TIME: 25 minutes
OVEN: 375°F

1 cooked pie shell
2 navel oranges, boiled
2 egg yolks, beaten
¾ cup sugar

To decorate
3 navel oranges
Apricot jam, melted

Purée the boiled oranges. Stir in the egg yolks and sugar. Slice the remaining three oranges. Fill the pie shell with the orange purée and decorate with slices of orange. Bake in a moderate oven until bubbling. Remove from oven and brush on melted apricot jam. Return to oven and bake for a further 10 minutes.

Fraises Escoffier

PREPARATION TIME: 15 minutes
plus chilling

2lb strawberries
2 oranges
2oz sugar cubes
⅓ cup Grand Marnier

Hull and slice the strawberries; peel and slice the oranges. Mash half the strawberries with the sugar cubes and Grand Marnier. Stir in the remaining fruit and chill for one hour. Serve in individual dishes.

Lemon Mousse

PREPARATION TIME: 6-10 minutes

¾ cup sugar
3 eggs, separated
5 lemons
1½ tablespoons gelatin
2 tablespoons warm water

Put the grated rind of the lemons in a basin with the egg yolks and sugar. Beat until stiff. Beat the egg whites until they peak. Dissolve the gelatin in the water and mix with the egg yolk mixture. Beat until the mixture begins to set. Fold in the egg whites. Fill the glasses with mousse. Serve chilled.

Fraises Escoffier (right), Orange Tart (center right) and Lemon Mousse (far right).

Strawberry Sauce

¼ cup sugar
1½ tablespoons lemon juice
1½ tablespoons brandy
9oz strawberries

Place sugar, lemon juice and brandy in a pan. Place over a low heat until sugar dissolves. Sieve strawberries to remove seeds and combine with syrup. Cool.

Caramel Chips

¼ cup superfine sugar

Put the sugar in a heavy saucepan and heat gently until the sugar liquifies and turns golden. Pour quickly onto foil and leave until cold. Break the chips with a rolling pin and use for decoration.

Apricot Purée

3 tablespoons sugar
1 tablespoon water
1 teaspoon lime juice
2 tablespoons apricot brandy
9oz well-ripened apricots

Combine sugar, water, lime juice and apricot brandy in pan. Dissolve sugar over low heat. Cool. Sieve or purée apricots in blender. Combine with syrup.

Chocolate Sauce

4oz dark chocolate
2 tablespoons milk
2 rounded tablespoons corn syrup

Melt the chocolate in a bowl over a pan of simmering water. Beat in the milk and corn syrup until glossy.

Sugar Syrup (medium syrup)

6 tablespoons sugar (granulated)
⅔ cup water

Boiling sugar for dessert making can easily be done without a thermometer. Mix together water and sugar in a small saucepan and boil until the mixture begins to thicken.

Index